CW00827935

"A WHITE BARBARIAN LADY"

*the story of Anne Noble,
a Victorian woman
imprisoned in China*

Liam D'Arcy-Brown

BRANDRAM

First published in Great Britain in 2016
by Brandram, an imprint of Takeaway (Publishing)

1st edition, v. 1.0 LS

Copyright © Liam D'Arcy-Brown 2016

Liam D'Arcy-Brown has asserted his right
to be identified as the author of this work

All rights reserved. No part of this publication may be reproduced,
stored in a retrieval system or transmitted in any form or by any means
without the prior written permission of the publisher nor be otherwise
circulated in any form of binding or cover other than that in which
it is published and without a similar condition being imposed on the
subsequent purchaser

Takeaway (Publishing), 33 New Street, Kenilworth CV8 2EY
books@takeawaypublishing.co.uk

British Library Cataloguing in Publication Data.
A catalogue record for this book is available from the British Library

ISBN 978-0-9931896-1-6

CONTENTS

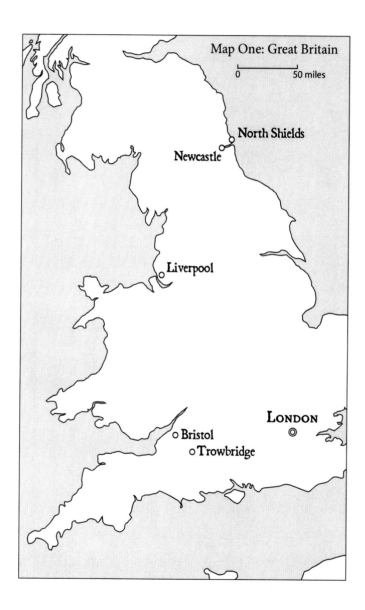

Map One: Great Britain

0   50 miles

North Shields

Newcastle

Liverpool

LONDON

Bristol

Trowbridge

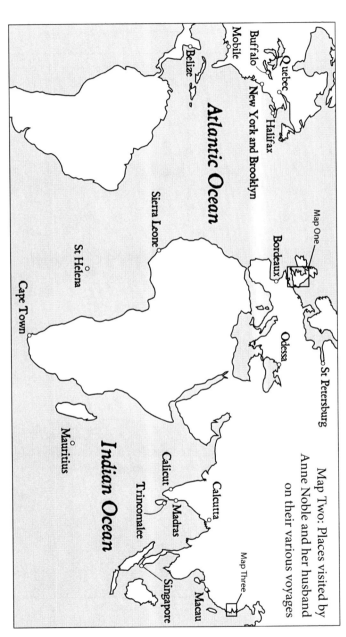

Map Two: Places visited by
Anne Noble and her husband
on their various voyages

Atlantic Ocean

Indian Ocean

Map One

Map Three

St Petersburg

Quebec
Buffalo
Mobile
New York and Brooklyn
Halifax
Belize

Bordeaux
Sierra Leone
St Helena
Cape Town
Odessa

Mauritius

Calicut
Trincomalee
Madras
Calcutta
Macau
Singapore

vi

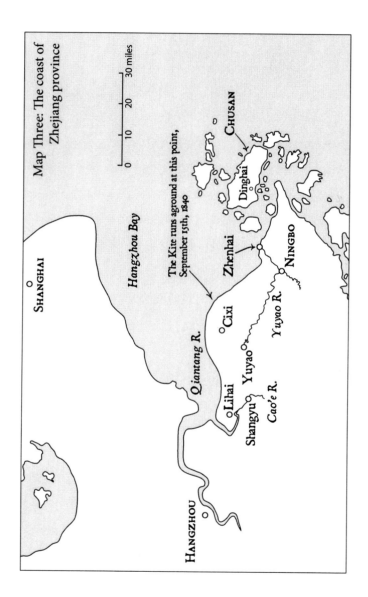

Map Three: The coast of Zhejiang province

0 10 20 30 miles

SHANGHAI

Hangzhou Bay

CHUSAN

Dinghai

The Kite runs aground at this point,
September 15th, 1840

Zhenhai

NINGBO

Qiantang R.

Cixi

Yuyao R.

Yuyao

Lihai

Shangyu

Cao'e R.

HANGZHOU

INTRODUCTION

ONE rainy autumn day in 1840, news began to spread along the coast of Hangzhou Bay that a foreign ship had foundered and that survivors had made it ashore, among them a young woman. Crowds turned out to see her, jeering as she was paraded barefoot and locked in a cage so tiny that her nose touched her knees.

Just a few months earlier, a shipwrecked foreign sailor would have been received so very differently; an object of intense curiosity, he would have been cared for and granted safe passage to his nearest compatriots, for these people respected the shifting sandbanks and fearsome currents of the East China Sea, and pitied men who had fallen foul of them. But these were far from normal times—China and Great Britain were at war. That summer, the British had attacked the island of Chusan and captured its walled city, Dinghai. With a fair wind, Chusan was just a few hours' sailing from that same stretch of coast where the *Kite* had run aground, and her crew could expect little sympathy now from a population bewildered and indignant at the violence being done to them. Their capture would affect the course of the war, handing the Chinese a vital bargaining chip that they were quick to exploit. A few days after the sinking of the *Kite*, the provincial governor addressed a letter to the commander of the British flotilla that lay at anchor off Chusan. It concerned a number of hostages the Chinese were holding:

> In all, we have captured more than twenty barbarian men, both white and black, and a white barbarian lady. They are all being treated well, and not in

the least harmed. If you, honourable admiral, will withdraw your men and ships and hand back the city of Dinghai, the imperial commissioner shall beg the great emperor's heavenly mercy that they be freed.

Sir Gordon Bremer was outraged, but he could only muster futile threats:

You call yourself a 'great nation', yet it is truly unworthy of the name to behave like this. If so much as one hair of their heads is harmed, then officers and men of this nation shall pour forth a righteous vengeance, wiping out the guilty and the innocent alike!

Who were these prisoners? he demanded to know. Urgungga replied in a calm and measured tone, well aware that fate had presented him with that most valuable of commodities—British hostages:

I have received your reply, asking for the names of the men and of the woman and the details of their capture, and requesting that they be freed. Your sentiments were most earnest, and I perceive that you are the kind of man who knows how to act according to changing circumstances. The woman's name is Anne Noble, and she is twenty-six years old.

Anne's surname would mislead the Chinese as to her status: she was not the noblewoman her gaolers believed her to be, but simply the wife of a sea-captain from Tyneside. She viewed her own life with equanimity: 'Death was nothing to me,' she would later write when recalling the events of her shipwreck and capture. 'I longed to be with my Saviour to praise him for ever, and to meet again my affectionate husband and sweet child, who were more than life to me.'

While in prison, Anne began to write a long letter to a confidante, a missionary's wife named Mrs Mary Gutzlaff who was residing some thirty miles away on Chusan:

> My ever dear friend. On Sunday, the 14th, I received your kind letter, containing the glad tidings of peace, and the joyful hope of a speedy release from prison; and in which you so sweetly and affectionately offer a home to the homeless. The Almighty alone, who searcheth the heart, knows how deeply grateful I feel for all your abundant goodness towards me in my great afflictions, but as my last letters were sent publicly, I could not express my feelings; I sincerely hope you have not thought me ungrateful. As I may now do so with safety, I will try to write to you the sad particulars of the dreadful wreck of the *Kite*, and of following events, as far as memory and the few notes I have been able to make from time to time, will enable me to do. May the Almighty in mercy strengthen me for the truly, melancholy duty. Amen. And I feel sure my dear friend, you will make due allowance for the state of mind in which I write.

We are fortunate that Anne recorded her experiences in her own words while she was still imprisoned, for we gain a very immediate impression of how she was able to make sense of—and ultimately survive—such a trauma. Her letter-writing was in fact interrupted by her release from prison, and she completed it on board the ship which was to carry her south to Macau. There it was swiftly put into print, and there can be no doubt that Anne herself was behind its publication; though it had been addressed to Mrs Gutzlaff, the intensely personal nature of the letter would have made it unthinkable for Mary to expose its contents to the world without Anne's say-so. In a private correspondence two years later, Anne was urged to take legal action against anybody who tried to reproduce her letter without her permission, which might make us suspect that its publication in Macau was partly by way of raising funds for herself. But even the ostensibly simple decision to produce a public account of her imprisonment must have been complicated by considerations of what constituted 'suitable' female behaviour in the 1840s. Here, we are also fortunate that attitudes toward women as writers had changed enormously over the preceding decades through the work of authors such as Fanny Burney, Elizabeth Hamilton, Mary Wollstonecraft, Susanna Rowson, Sydney Owenson, Mary Shelley, and many others.

By way of an example of the literary context within which Anne's letter was to appear, in 1817 there went on sale a work entitled *Original Letters from India, containing a Narrative of a Journey through Egypt, and the Author's Imprisonment at Calicut*. The author, a Mrs Eliza Fay, had touched at Calicut on the Malabar Coast in 1779 while travelling to Calcutta with her husband. Seized by the Sultan of Mysore, they had 'for fifteen weeks endured all the hardships and privations of a rigorous emprisonment'. But the letters relating her experiences which Eliza wrote to a friend lay unpublished for four decades, because, according to the preface of her book,

> at this period a woman who was not conscious of possessing decided genius or superior knowledge could not easily be induced to leave 'the harmless tenor of her way', and render herself amenable to the 'pains and penalties' then, generally, inflicted on female authorships; unless inspired by that enthusiasm that tramples on difficulties, or goaded by misfortune which admits not of alternative.

However,

> Since then, a considerable change has gradually taken place in public sentiments, and we have now not only as in former days a number of women who do honour to their sex as literary characters, but many unpretending females, who fearless of the critical perils that once attended the voyage, venture to launch their little barks on the vast ocean through which amusement or instruction is conveyed to a reading public.... A female author is no longer regarded as an object of derision.

So it is likely that Anne did not feel any great obligation to keep her writings private out of feminine respectability. In fact, given that the literary genre of what might be called 'narratives of suffering' was well established by the 1840s, she might even have felt that the publication of her letter was, as she said, a 'duty', and positively to be desired.

For as Europeans pushed ever further into unfamiliar parts of the globe, it was inevitable that a proportion of them would meet with unpleasantness, and their stories were eagerly read. In 1805, for example, a book whose title was almost as long as its contents (it was just eight pages) was printed in London:

> *An Affecting Narrative of the Sufferings of Six Soldiers who deserted from the garrison of St Helena, in an open boat, with only a small quantity of bread and water. After being driven about at sea, for near a month, they were forced by dreadful sufferings and hunger to draw lots which of them should kill himself to preserve the rest from starving, and they were forced to eat human flesh.*

As printing became cheaper and easier, reprints of earlier stories were reissued, for example the 1812 *Narrative of the Sufferings of Eight English Seamen, left by accident in Greenland in the year 1630*, and the 1828 *Narrative of the Captivity, Sufferings, and Removes, of Mrs Mary Rowlandson who was taken by the Indians at the Destruction of Lancaster in 1676*. The ill-treatment of such Europeans at the hands of implicitly uncivilised peoples abounded: a year after Mrs Fay's *Original Letters* were published, *A Narrative of my Captivity in Japan during the years 1811, 1812 and 1813* went on sale, written by a captain of the Royal Navy.

Soon, the most common scene of suffering was the westward-expanding United States. Who could fail to be moved by *An Affecting Narrative of the Captivity and Sufferings of Mrs Mary Smith: who, with her husband and three daughters, were taken prisoners by the Indians in August last and after enduring the most cruel hardships and torture of mind for sixty days (in which time she witnessed the tragical death of her husband and helpless children) was fortunately rescued from the merciless hands of the savages*, or *A Narrative of the Captivity of Mrs Horn, and her two children, with Mrs Harris, by the Camanache Indians after they had murdered their husbands and travelling companions (with a brief account of the manners and customs of that nation of savages, of whom so little is generally known)*? It's quite possible that Anne, who as we shall see had spent time in the US, was familiar with accounts such as these.

Of course, as men, Anne's fellow prisoners did not need to consider the respectability or otherwise of giving an account of their experiences in China, and we are immensely fortunate that with their writings we can corroborate Anne's story and flesh out the details of her day-to-day life. A short letter written by an English naval lieutenant who had been on the *Kite*, for example, made its way into the *Singapore Free Press*; a doctor of the Madras Army, in his own account of the war, reprinted a letter written by an artillery captain imprisoned alongside Anne; most astonishingly of all, several dozen of the rice-paper notes that passed furtively between the cells in Ningbo gaol survived the passing of 170 years. But by far the most comprehensive account of the sinking of the *Kite* and the conditions in which Mrs Noble was held comes from an apprentice mariner named John Lee Scott.

Scott, who hailed originally from Southgate in Middlesex, was just nineteen years old when he was captured by the Chinese. Arriving back in England six months after being released, he wasted no time in writing his *Narrative of a Recent Imprisonment in China after the Wreck of the Kite.* At some 23,000 words, his account is three times the length of Anne's and written for very different reasons. Where Anne dwells upon the emotional effects of imprisonment and upon the relationships—both temporal and spiritual—that sustained her, John Lee Scott is inquisitive, fascinated by the unfamiliar details of his surroundings, and keenly observant of cultural differences. Setting down her ordeal in writing was clearly a form of catharsis for Anne; Scott, however, for all the suffering he recounts, evidently looked back on aspects of his captivity as rather an adventure. He must, after all, have gone to sea in the knowledge that life might be dangerous, but in the hope nevertheless that it might be exciting. Not for a moment do we ever get the impression that Anne enjoyed anything of her time in Ningbo. A young woman who had borne two children, in her letter to Mary Gutzlaff she was confiding in a kindred soul—the middle-aged wife of a Protestant missionary and the adoptive mother of a brood of Chinese orphans. Middle-class Victorian women such as these were defined by their matrimonial and maternal status, and

Anne time and again sets her experiences in China against these twin domestic roles. Where John Lee Scott must have been able to imagine a life for himself after (and if) he was released, able still to earn his living as a sailor, Anne could only see her future (if indeed God wished her to survive her immediate situation) as one of destitution. Unmarried, she would like any other Englishwoman of her class have lived under her parents' roof; married, her welfare had become her husband's responsibility. But in Ningbo she was as far as could possibly be imagined from the feminine ideals of hearth and home. There was no trailblazing role-model nor heroine whose persona might have given some meaning to her suffering; Anne's instinctive and immediate role-model was Christ, in particular the suffering Christ of Gethsemane who prayed that God's will be done. Indeed, to the modern reader the most conspicuous aspect of Anne's character to come across in her letter is this profound faith that God was directing the events of her life, and that only by trusting in Divine Providence would she be enabled to understand and accept His purposes. Ever present is Anne's certainty that suffering was to be endured on the path to salvation, and embraced as a sign that God had plans for her: 'The Almighty alone knows the reason why he afflicted us,' she wrote, 'and I fervently hope that these many solemn warnings may be sanctified to us.'

While the teenage sailor John Lee Scott only once gives us any hint that he resorted to prayer, we can scarcely read two consecutive paragraphs of Anne's letter without her expressing the most heartfelt gratitude for the blessings God has shown her. It is a testament to her character and faith that Anne concluded with

> a sincere, solemn, and heartfelt ascription of praise
> and thanks to the Almighty Father, the Gracious
> Saviour and the all-sustaining Spirit, who has so truly

fulfilled his promise, 'I will not leave thee, nor forsake thee.'

But if Anne was every bit the Christian woman we would not be overly surprised to find in early Victorian England, other aspects of her life are decidedly unexpected.

In an age when we think nothing of flying between continents, it's easy to assume that our Victorian ancestors must have shrunk from what were then long and dangerous journeys and instead spent their lives within much more confined horizons. As anybody who has traced their family tree will appreciate, however, the idea that people in Anne's day rarely strayed far beyond the town they were born is very much mistaken. At a very conservative estimate, Anne could not have travelled less than 120,000 miles during her lifetime, crossing and recrossing the Atlantic, Pacific, and Indian oceans, and there's no reason to doubt that she made other long voyages we know nothing about. Her husband James sailed even further during his far shorter life, and many of Anne's immediate relations—including her elderly mother—crossed the Atlantic time and again, with two of her brothers even emigrating to Australia.

And the background to Anne's imprisonment in Ningbo even reveals that she was far from being the only woman present to witness the events of the First Opium War. Officers, soldiers, sailors, merchants, missionaries, and others—all arrived on the China coast bringing with them wives and families. When the troopship *Belleisle* left England, for example, she had aboard her 41 women and no fewer than 75 children, stringing sheets between the hulls to afford themselves a little privacy. Rather than being a lone female with only male companionship, we discover that Anne was supported during her imprisonment by other women who rallied to comfort her, if only from a distance. So how on earth had this young Englishwoman ended up in China, what happened to her there, and what became of her?

1

millworkers and mariners

ANNE'S childhood home in Trowbridge, the county
town of Wiltshire, could scarcely have been more
different from the teeming cities of Qing-dynasty China.[1]
The baptismal register of St James' parish church records
that she was christened Mary Ann Watson on June 7th,
1814, though she seems always to have gone by her middle
name.

Wandering the rolling farmland around Trowbridge
today, with its peaceful villages of honey-coloured stone,
it is hard to imagine that in the early nineteenth century
this corner of England was at the forefront of the Industrial Revolution. Since the Middle Ages the town had
prospered on the quality of its fine woollen cloth, finished
to the highest standards by spinners and weavers who
worked their looms by hand. Then in the 1790s the rumble
of machinery began to be heard, first for combing the wool
and spinning it, then for raising the nap and shearing the
cloth. Water-power replaced the handlooms, and then,
when the efforts of the slow-moving River Biss had been
outstripped, steam replaced water. In 1814, the same year
Anne was born, the first Boulton & Watt steam engine was
erected in a Trowbridge cloth mill. Fuel arrived on the new
Somerset Coal Canal, and with the Kennet and Avon Canal
soon completed right on the town's doorstep barges could
travel non-stop between the ports of Bristol and London
and output surged.

Anne's father Thomas Watson, a native of the nearby market town of Melksham, became one of the many who went to Trowbridge to find work. There in 1804, aged twenty, he married a Wiltshire girl, Susannah Grigory, and two years later a son was born. Before Anne was born in 1814, Susannah had given birth to at least four children—William, Elvira, James, and Sarah—and five more would follow—Henry, Thomas, Susannah, Olivia, and Benjamin—the last of them in 1830, by which time his eldest sibling William was already in his early twenties. In an age of high infant mortality, there might well have been other children who did not survive long enough to leave a record in the church register.

We cannot say for certain how Thomas and Susannah earned a living during their early married life in Hill Street, but the greater part of Trowbridge's population—men, women, and children alike—were employed in the weaving industry, either in the mills or by doing piece-work at home. The early years of the nineteenth century were a fine time to be in cloth: the Napoleonic Wars had broken out the year before Thomas and Susannah wed, vastly increasing the demand for uniforms as the British army swelled to some quarter of a million men. When the first national census was recorded in 1841, the Watsons were living in better accommodation in Fore Street and Thomas was working as a 'slubber', looking after the machines that would put the first twist into the drawn-out fleece in preparation for spinning. By then in his mid-fifties, he would have spent his entire working life in one mill or another and would have been reasonably comfortable—not poor, but certainly far from wealthy. It is mentioned in passing in an edition of the *Bristol Mercury* the following year that Thomas was 'in the employ of Messrs. Stancomb of Trowbridge'.[2] The Stancombs were an important name in the Trowbridge weaving industry (there is a Stancomb Avenue in memory of them) and Thomas must have been working in one of the family's three mills, most likely for one James Stancomb, whose steam-driven mill specialised in 'scribbling, carding and slubbing' the raw wool as the first stage of producing a fine, twill cloth known as 'kerseymere'.[3]

What was life like there? A Royal Commission of 1833 into the conditions in just such a textile mill heard evidence from one young man on life under a slubber like Thomas Watson.[4] Matthew Crabtree had started at the age of eight, often being lifted out of bed by his parents while still asleep, before running two miles to the mill to work fifteen hours every day. Physical chastisement was not unknown: 'Do you think,' Matthew was asked, 'that if the overlooker were naturally a humane person it would still be found necessary for him to beat the children, in order to keep up their attention and vigilance at the termination of those extraordinary days of labour?'

> Yes. The machine turns off a regular quantity of cardings, and of course, they must keep as regularly to their work the whole of the day. They must keep up with the machine, and therefore however humane the slubber may be, as he must keep up with the machine or be found fault with, he spurs the children to keep up also by various means but that which he commonly resorts to is to strap them when they become drowsy.

That life in the Trowbridge mills was much the same is clear from the written answers the Stancombs gave to the Royal Commission. They employed children as young as seven and a half for something between nine and fourteen hours a day, five and a half days every week. Corporal punishment, the Stancombs readily admitted, could be meted out by overlookers—such as was Thomas Watson—using 'a small stick or strap'.[5] It's probable, then, that Anne's own father was obliged to be such a man if he was to keep his job. Yet Thomas, holding a position of responsibility, must surely have wanted to protect his own children from the harshest of conditions. Of Anne's childhood we have scarcely any firm details, but where Matthew Crabtree paints a picture of a childhood that consisted of little more than sleep and work, the vocabulary, elegance, and religious sentiment of Anne's writings do not seem to be those of a woman who had spent her formative years working at a loom to the detriment of her education. In 1812, the National Society for Promoting the Education of the Poor in the Principles of the Established Church had opened a school in Trowbridge.[6] There, for five hours a day for three years, with holidays only at Christmas and harvest, boys and girls alike were taught reading, writing, and arithmetic, instructed in the catechism of the Church of England, and required to attend regular church services. Girls, in addition, were taught needlework.[7]

Whether or not Anne learned to sew at the Trowbridge National School or at her mother's side as a piece-worker, by the age of eighteen she was working as a dressmaker, for this is how she described herself when in 1833 she travelled to Bristol with her younger sister Susannah and with ninety-two other passengers boarded the ship *Earl Grey* bound for New York. By then, a Wiltshire weaving industry which had been booming only twenty years earlier had started its terminal decline, overtaken by the more productive mill towns of Yorkshire and Lancashire. Anne's elder brother James, a tailor, had already made the journey (the 1855 State Census records that he had by then been living in New York for 23 years) and they had presumably corresponded on the opportunities that America offered.

With almost two centuries of hindsight, we can see one intriguing similarity between the town of Trowbridge which Anne now left behind and the otherwise utterly dissimilar city of New York: this was the era of canal-building, and just as Trowbridge had flourished after the digging of the Somerset Coal Canal and the Kennet and Avon, so New York too had boomed as the Atlantic terminus of the Erie Canal that eight years earlier had linked the Hudson to the Great Lakes. Immigration through the port of New York swelled as populations headed inland to Buffalo, and from there to the Midwest. The writer Ralph Waldo Emerson, crossing the Atlantic to New York in the same year as Anne and Susannah, described the passage as 'very long, crooked, rough, and eminently disagreeable': this was not a trip one took for pleasure, and the Watson sisters must have expected that the outlay in time and money (a steerage ticket cost in the region of £4) would prove worthwhile.[8] And in a sense, it did: whatever her reason for being there, it was in New York that Anne was to meet her future husband.

Quite unlike Anne, James Smith Noble came from a seafaring family and was thoroughly at home aboard a ship. Eighteen years older than his future wife, he had been born in 1796 to the master mariner Ralph Noble and his wife Ann in Shadwell, on the north shore of the Thames a mile or so east of the City of London. Shadwell had changed beyond recognition in the decades before James Noble's birth: in the 1720s (when, incidentally, President Thomas Jefferson's mother Jane Randolph was born there) it had been a mere hamlet; by the 1790s it was a dense tangle of streets and alleyways encroaching ever more into the surrounding fields. During James's childhood the area was to see even greater changes, its early wharves and slipways vanishing beneath the purpose-built London Docks that handled cargoes from across a burgeoning Empire.

James Noble was the second of six children, and his early years were spent living in the narrow streets that led down to the Thames' foreshore. Before James was ten years of age, however, we find in *Holden's Directory* of London businesses that his father Ralph had become a ship's captain and that the family had moved to the salubrity of a newly-built house in Clark's Terrace, a comfortable distance from the grime of the river.[9] To judge from subsequent issues of *Holden's Directory*, Ralph evidently progressed from ship's captain to shipowner, possibly of the brig *Noble* that plied the North Sea route between London and Tyneside, from where his family originally hailed.[10] But in 1810 Ralph's good fortune changed overnight with the death of his wife Ann at the age of just thirty-seven, 'most sincerely beloved and regretted by her family and friends'.[11] Things rapidly went from bad to worse for the Nobles: Ralph was no longer a shipowner but instead just a 'merchant, dealer and chapman' when in the following year a notice in *Jackson's Oxford Journal* announced that he was bankrupt;[12] speculating on shipping and cargoes was a risky undertaking at the best of times, and the loss of his spouse and mother of his children, the youngest aged just six, would have made life terribly hard. Unable to repay his creditors, Ralph quickly found himself in one of London's cramped and unsanitary debtors' prisons, and five years after his discharge in 1813 he too was dead.[13]

So by the age of twenty-three James Noble had lost both his parents. What effect those bereavements had upon him at a personal level we cannot say, as no personal letters or diaries have survived; yet despite his loss he did follow in his father's footsteps to become an experienced sea-captain. Whether or not he had command of a vessel in the years following his father's death is also now impossible to confirm: the common surname 'Noble' appears far too frequently in *Lloyd's Register of British & Foreign Shipping* for us to be sure, and at any one time there were always several different ships operating out of English ports under the command of a 'J. Noble' or even a 'James Noble'—the *Liverpool Mercury* of June 21st, 1816, for example, carries an advertisement for sailings to New York on the ship *Herald*, 'James Noble, Master'. During the mid-1820s, our particular James Noble might have been the man of that name commanding the *Friendship*, the *Platoff*, the *Cassiope*, the *Harmony*, the *Sylvan*, or many other a vessel, or none at all. But whatever the truth of James' employment during the 1810s and 1820s, there is plenty of evidence to show that during the early 1830s he was in command of a merchantman named the *Miriam & Jane*.

When in 1830 the *Miriam & Jane* docked at Newcastle with a temporary skipper—her captain, John Smith, had drowned while trying to go ashore in Canada—James must have jumped at the chance to step into his shoes: barque-rigged sailing ships such as she were the ocean-going workhorses of their day, capable of speeds that challenged those of the more labour-intensive full-rigged ships with their cumbersome square sails, but needing far fewer crewmen. It's fitting, then, that another technical innovation in our own day has allowed us to piece together the voyages of the *Miriam & Jane* at a speed that would have been unthinkable just a few years ago.

The digitization of thousands of local and national newspapers, and their availability on the internet, has turned what used to be months of travelling and of trawling through archives into the work of a few hours at a computer. In the *Newcastle Courant* of September 18th, 1830, for example, under the heading *Marine Intelligence* we find an entry reading simply 'Miriam and Jane, Noble, Cronstadt', this being one of several dozen vessels which had cleared customs at Newcastle and sailed for foreign ports during the previous week. For the next three years, the voyages of the *Miriam & Jane* can be followed in James's local *Newcastle Courant* and in other newspapers—the *Newcastle Journal*, London's *Standard*, the *Morning Post*, and more—as she sailed to St Petersburg on the Baltic and to Odessa on the Black Sea before crossing the Atlantic to Quebec and then shuttling back and forth between Newcastle, Canada, and New England, bringing back cargoes of timber from the New World to the Old. Though they were by necessity reduced to the barest essentials of ports and dates in the newspapers' regular shipping columns, each of his voyages was lengthy and demanding, and some of them ended badly. When this was the case, we invariably find the events recounted in detail—just as today, a single shipwreck was more newsworthy than a thousand safe voyages. In the *Caledonian Mercury*, for example, we read that in the winter of 1832, while anchored off the town of Rimouski on the St Lawrence River, the *Miriam & Jane* was driven by ice and wind onto the tiny Barnaby Island. James, along with the ship's carpenter and a crewman, went ashore but were left stranded until they could be rescued. (To a landsman's eyes, indeed, the *Miriam & Jane* might easily appear to be a most ill-starred vessel: one previous winter she had got ashore in the Firth of Forth and was leaking badly when she finally made it into harbour. In truth, running aground was an occupational hazard of seafaring, and was very common.)[14] Then in April of the following year, 1833, according to the *Liverpool Mercury* the *Miriam & Jane* yet again ran aground, this time at the entrance to Mobile Bay, Alabama, losing her anchor, cable, and rudder.[15] But it was this fortuitous accident that was to bring James and his future wife together: after doing enough work to render her seaworthy, he sailed the *Miriam & Jane* north to New York, where he docked on May 14th.[16] The damage to the *Miriam & Jane* must have been considerable, since she was laid over in New York for more than two months before taking to the seas once more. As a consequence, James was still in the city when, on June 3rd, Anne Watson stepped off the *Earl Grey* and onto American soil.

Family tradition among Anne's descendants long had it that James and Anne met at a 'church social' in Brooklyn, fell in love, and married in Trinity Church, Manhattan. But the family's oral history was only committed to paper in the twentieth century by Anne's great-granddaughter Mary Tower Buffum, and after the passage of time the details could not be confirmed. This remained the case until 2015, when an obscure publication was digitized and put online. The survival of *The Christian Intelligencer*, and with it the only evidence of James and Anne's marriage, is remarkable: there was no legal requirement in New York back then to keep a record of marriages, and the church registers are all too often incomplete or missing. So we are astonishingly fortunate that when, in 1830, the Reformed Dutch Church of New York City began publishing *The Christian Intelligencer*, they decided to include announcements of marriages performed not only by ministers of their own church but also any others that came to the editor's attention. And this is how we can say for certain that 'Captain James Noble and Miss Mary Ann Watson' were joined in holy matrimony by the Reverend F. H. Cuming on July 20th, 1833, in the old Grace Church, Manhattan.[17] The mistaken family tradition is quite understandable: before a new site was found two miles to the north, Grace Church used to stand facing Trinity Church on the corner

The neoclassical Grace Church on Broadway (with tower and cupola), where Anne and James married on July 20th, 1833 (from *The Picture of New-York*, 1828).

of Broadway and Rector Street, in what today is the heart of the city's financial district.

Given that Anne had arrived in New York on June 3rd, she could not possibly have known James for anything more than six weeks—and that at the very most!—before promising to spend the rest of her life with him. To modern sensibilities, a marriage so soon after a first meeting would seem impetuous, but courtship in the mid-nineteenth century could be very swift indeed: James would not have known when—or if—any of his future trips might bring him back to New York, and whether he might ever see Anne again. It would have been unthinkable for them to have begun a sexual relationship before marriage, or even, given what we can infer about Anne's moral sensibilities, to have been alone together before a formal engagement; and to have left New York on James's ship without being his wife would have been scandalous. James had already spent longer in New York than he would normally have done, and time was money. The simple need to get another profitable voyage under way once more might have lain behind their decision to marry as soon as possible rather than part company, as just two days after their wedding the *Miriam & Jane* sailed north for Halifax, Nova Scotia.[18] Since there is no record of James or his ship ever revisiting

New York, we can reasonably assume that Anne was with him on the *Miriam & Jane* from this point on.

Despite modern portrayals of olden-day sailors as a super-stitious lot, for a sea-captain's wife to accompany her husband like this was not at all remarkable and was, indeed, a matter of indifference to a crew; in fact, a previous master of the very same *Miriam & Jane* had enjoyed the company of his wife, sister, and children on board (their presence had only come to the attention of the outside world when one day in 1826 the ship rolled onto her side while taking on ballast in Quebec, leading to shrieks from the terrified womenfolk!).[19] The memoirs of Abby Morrell, wife to the captain of a New England whaler and a contemporary of Anne, casts light on Anne's decision to follow James to sea rather than wait for him on dry land:

> Although I knew when I married him I was to be the wife of a seafaring man it was impossible for me as a fifteen-year-old bride to realise the distress of separation. Barely three weeks had passed [after our marriage] when on 18 July [1824] his voyage began, and for many nights my dreams were only of him being tossed by storms, engulfed in the deep, or wrecked on desolate isles subjected to the violence of savages. He has good sailors with him, said my friends, but good sailors are not the same as a good wife, I thought. In this manner passed my nights and days, until he returned on 9 May 1826, two months short of two years, when my happiness was again complete.[20]

When in 1828 her husband had again sailed for the South Seas, Abby had missed him so much that she determined to accompany him from then on: 'At first he would not hear of it, but when I insisted (as far as affectionate obedience could insist) he at last reluctantly yielded, and once agreed he put the best side outwards.' Her husband's reluctance to have Abby aboard was simply out of concern for her wellbeing, not out of fear that, Jonah-like, she would endanger the *Antarctic*. Likewise with Anne, it's clear from the affection with which she would later write of her husband that she was deeply in love with him, and her decision to be with him aboard the *Miriam & Jane* is not to be wondered at. And by way of illustrating the varying attitudes of Anne's near-contemporaries toward women and seafaring, it's worthwhile citing from the dining-room scene at the Musgroves' home in Jane Austen's *Persuasion*.

> [Admiral Croft to Captain Wentworth] 'If you had been a week later at Lisbon, last spring, Frederick, you would have been asked to give a passage to Lady Mary Grierson and her daughters.'
>
> 'Should I? I am glad I was not a week later then.'
>
> The admiral abused him for his want of gallantry. He defended himself: though professing that he would never willingly admit any ladies on board a ship of his, excepting for a ball, or a visit, which a few hours might comprehend.
>
> 'But, if I know myself,' said he, 'this is from no want of gallantry towards them. It is rather from feeling how impossible it is, with all one's efforts, and all one's sacrifices, to make the accommodations on board such as women ought to have. There can be no want of gallantry, Admiral, in rating the claims of women to every personal comfort *high*, and this is what I do. I hate to hear of women on board, or to see them on board; and no ship, under my command, shall ever convey a family of ladies anywhere, if I can help it.'

This brought his sister [Mrs Sophia Croft] upon him. 'Oh! Frederick! But I cannot believe it of you. All idle refinement! Women may be as comfortable on board, as in the best house in England. I believe I have lived as much on board as most women, and I know nothing superior to the accommodations of a man-of-war. I declare I have not a comfort or an indulgence about me ... beyond what I always had in most of the ships I have lived in; and they have been five altogether.'

'Nothing to the purpose,' replied her brother. 'You were living with your husband, and were the only woman on board.'

'But you, yourself, brought Mrs Harville, her sister, her cousin, and the three children, round from Portsmouth to Plymouth. Where was this superfine, extraordinary sort of gallantry of yours then?'

'All merged in my friendship, Sophia. I would assist any brother-officer's wife that I could, and I would bring any thing of Harville's from the world's end, if he wanted it. But do not imagine that I did not feel it an evil in itself.'

'Depend upon it, they were all perfectly comfortable.'

'I might not like them the better for that, perhaps. Such a number of women and children have no *right* to be comfortable on board.'

'My dear Frederick, you are talking quite idly. Pray, what would become of us poor sailors' wives, who often want to be conveyed to one port or another, after our husbands, if everybody had your feelings?'

'What a great traveller you must have been, ma'am!' said Mrs Musgrove to Mrs Croft.

'Pretty well, ma'am, in the fifteen years of my marriage; though many women have done more. I have crossed the Atlantic four times, and have been once to the East Indies and back again, and only once; besides being in different places about home: Cork, and Lisbon, and Gibraltar. But I never went beyond the Straits, and never was in the West Indies. ... And I do assure you, ma'am, that nothing can exceed the accommodations of a man-of-war; I speak, you know, of the higher rates. When you come to a frigate, of course, you are more confined; though any reasonable woman may be perfectly happy in one of them; and I can safely say, that the happiest part of my life has been spent on board a ship. ... A little disordered always the first twenty-four hours of going to sea, but never knew what sickness was afterwards. The only time that I ever really suffered in body or mind, the only time that I ever fancied myself unwell, or had any ideas of danger, was the winter that I passed by myself at Deal, when the Admiral (*Captain* Croft then) was in the North Seas. I lived in perpetual fright at that time, and had all manner of imaginary complaints from not knowing what to do with myself, or when I should hear from him next; but as long as we could be together, nothing ever ailed me, and I never met with the smallest inconvenience.'

It is abundantly clear from Anne's letters that, just like Mrs Croft, she was very much in love with her husband, and it should come as no surprise that she chose a life aboard ship with James rather than spend months or years separated from him.

After taking Anne as both helpmeet and shipmate, James widened his horizons and began to sail even further afield, and from the newspapers' shipping intelligence columns of the day we can again follow them. In 1834 the *Miriam & Jane* sailed to Sierra Leone in West Africa, picking up a cargo of teak and canewood and carrying it back to Britain. By the end of the same year the Nobles had crossed the Atlantic to the Honduras, loaded the *Miriam & Jane* with 340 mahogany logs, and brought them back to Liverpool. But on their third trip together disaster struck. On September 3rd, 1835, the *Miriam & Jane* had left the Honduras once more and was sailing for Ireland with a further cargo of mahogany when—for the fourth time since being laid down in 1824—she ran aground, this final time at Caye Caulker, one of the string of coral islands off the coast of modern-day Belize. Though her cargo was salvaged and her crew saved, the *Miriam & Jane* was lost.

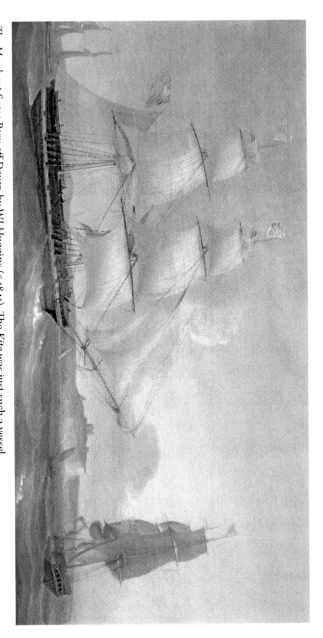

The Merchant Snow Peru off Dover, by WJ Huggins (c.1841). The *Kite* was just such a vessel.

2

the Kite

HOW James and Anne recrossed the Atlantic from the Caribbean back to England is a mystery. The next detail we can be sure of is that their first child, Ann Fenwick Noble (she was known as Annie, presumably to distinguish her from her mother), was born on September 8th, 1837, in North Shields, the fishing port that commands the left bank of the Tyne as it opens into the North Sea. Their decision to set up home there was understandable: though James's late father Ralph had married, raised a family, and died on the banks of the Thames, he was a native of Tyneside. With his own parents both dead and his late father's extended family still living in North Shields, a return to his father's hometown would have offered kinship and economic security after losing everything he owned in the Gulf of Honduras.

James seems to have given up skippering for the duration of Annie's early infancy: from the loss of the *Miriam & Jane* in 1835 through to his next appointment in 1838 his name doesn't appear in the comprehensive *Lloyd's Register*. His next—and sadly his last—captaincy was to be of the brig *Kite*, laid down by the shipwrights Thomas and William Smith, specialists in East India vessels who were renowned for building some of the finest of their kind. The *Kite* was completed in the middle of 1837, her progress from bare keel to seaworthy hull having taken shape in St Peter's Dock, Newcastle, a short distance upriver from North

Shields, at just the same time as Anne's first pregnancy was proceeding. Technically she was a 'snow brig', with a small, third mast fitted to the rear of her mainmast. This 'snow mast' allowed her to fly a hindmost sail that could move freely, unconstrained by the yardarms of the mainmast. Such a neat design made her faster and more manoeuverable. Her hull was sheathed in copper to keep shipworm and seaweed at bay, and at 281 tons she was bigger than most brigs (yet still some 30 tons lighter than the *Miriam & Jane*).

The *Kite* took her first oceanic voyage in 1838. Rather than make his familiar 12,000-mile return crossing of the Atlantic to Central America, though, James instead bore south around Cape Finisterre and sailed to Bordeaux to pick up a consignment of wine. From Bordeaux the *Kite* sailed for Singapore (the young British colony was 'one of the most delightful little places I saw,' said Mrs Morrell when her ship anchored there in 1831), calling on the return leg at the island of Mauritius. (It is likely, during the several weeks in which the *Kite* was laid over there in Port Louis, that Anne visited the grave of Harriet Newell, the American missionary who had died on the island twenty years earlier, aged just nineteen; Harriet's *Memoirs* were still popular and instructive reading, and Anne was a particularly pious Christian.) From Mauritius, the *Kite* returned to Tyneside by way of a long detour via Madras and Calcutta, both of which were under British administration. The entire voyage had covered some 35,000 miles, and there is no reason to doubt that Anne was aboard her for the entire fifteen months, turning twenty-four years of age while the *Kite* was at anchor in the June heat of Singapore.

On Monday, July 8th, 1839, James and Anne left Tyneside for the last time and headed once more for Bordeaux to pick up wine for Mauritius. Rather than take little Annie with them, they chose to leave her in North Shields in the care of James' older sister Isabella.[1] Whether Anne was carrying a second child at this point is unclear: she might have decided to leave Annie behind rather than nurse two infants at once aboard a ship; or she might already have handed Annie over to Isabella's safekeeping for the *Kite*'s 1838 voyage and for this voyage likewise, not thinking herself pregnant. Either way, a son—they named him Ralph after James' late father—was born sometime in the spring of 1840.

What, then, was life at sea like for a woman such as Anne? The rather derisive term 'hen frigate' is sometimes said to have been used of a ship whose captain had his wife living on board:[2] the compiler of the contemporary *Dictionary of the Vulgar Tongue* even joked that such a woman was said to be in command. Yet apart from this rare mention, 'hen frigate' is conspicuously hard to find in the writings of the day.[3] The fact that reference was made without the least implication of distaste to wives and children being present on warships and transports during the *Kite*'s time at sea is good evidence that women could accompany their menfolk without attracting any overt disapproval. There were certainly other women living aboard ships on the Zhejiang coast during the subsequent hostilities between Great Britain and China: when HMS *Rattlesnake* one day opened fire, Mrs Bull the boatswain's wife was found hiding belowdecks, terrified by the noise.

Anne was the only woman aboard the *Kite*, and unlike each and every male member of the crew she had no allotted role. Unable to help with the most physically demanding skills needed to man a snow-brig—setting and stowing the heavy canvas sails, bracing the yards, pumping the bilges, weighing the anchor, casting the lead, and so on—she would have taken on what was seen on land as 'women's work'. Besides washing the laundry and possibly helping the cook to prepare meals, Anne would have passed much of her time in reading—merchant ships of the day often carried extensive collections of books to help while away the months at sea. She was an intelligent and numerate woman, and her husband possibly taught her to calculate the ship's position with sextant and chronometer. The cabin she shared with James would have been cramped, something in the order of two or three yards square, and with just enough headroom to stand upright. Its furniture would have consisted of little more than a desk, a chair, and a bed. And it can only be hoped that it was a comfortable bed, as Anne must have given birth upon it.

We don't know precisely where the *Kite* was when Anne went into labour, as the ship's log was lost when it sank. But the newspaper shipping reports do survive and we know that the *Kite* called at Mauritius in March of 1840 before arriving in Madras on April 2nd, spending nine days there before sailing for Trincomalee in Ceylon. The only clue we have to baby Ralph's date of birth is that the sailor John Lee Scott thought he was 'about five months old' by the late summer of 1840 (though teenage boys are not necessarily the most interested observers of newborn children!). This would place his arrival sometime in the early spring, possibly at anchor but most likely somewhere in the Indian Ocean. If the *Kite* had been in harbour, Anne's husband James would have been able to find a European doctor or another captain's wife to assist at the birth; if at sea, Anne would have had to trust in her husband and to God. James must have known for many months that Anne was pregnant and that they might soon have an infant to feed, and it is possible that the *Kite* carried a nanny-goat, given that there was no guarantee that Anne would be able to produce enough breastmilk. (There were other ways of feeding babies on board ship, too: the wife of an American whaling captain wrote in 1867 that she was giving her child 'rice water sweetened with sugar, with what milk I can give her', while another woman crushed up ship's biscuits and mixed them with water.)[4] Between sea-sickness, pregnancy, the pain of labour, and the strain of nursing a crying baby, and with the heat of the tropics and a husband who was obliged to pay more attention to his ship and crew than to his wife, her last long sea-voyage as a married woman could not have been a particularly pleasurable one for poor Anne.

When James and Anne set sail from Tyneside in July of 1839 they would have been aware of the hostile atmosphere prevailing on the China coast. Just a month earlier, the Nobles' local newspaper the *Newcastle Courant* had carried the latest from Canton, where British traders were still offering opium for sale despite the Chinese authorities' best efforts to ban its import:

> It appears that the Chinese government is taking effectual measures to put down the smuggling of opium into its dominions. A great deal of excitement prevails in consequence of this decision, and determination to carry it into execution, as it cuts up a trade attended with great profit, and in which many British merchants have participated for fifty years.[5]

More than once the hostility had even tipped over into violence, with cannon-fire exchanged between British ships and Chinese customs-vessels. The English newspapers regularly carried reports on the opium trade and on China's efforts to put an end to it, and when James and Anne had visited Singapore a year earlier they would have heard first-hand the latest word from the captains of opium clippers returning to Calcutta. Had they consulted *Moore's Almanack* to see what it prophesied, they would have seen its clear warning to 'Look again at the horrors of the *opium trade* in China, and watch the dealings of Providence with that country *and the British residents there!*'. But by 1839 it would in truth have required no great prophetic gift to have sensed that Britain and China were perilously close to all-out war.

To give a full account of the diplomatic and commercial dealings which went on between Great Britain and the Qing dynasty from the start of the eighteenth century until the outbreak of war would require several volumes in itself; even then, the possible angles from which the roots of the First Opium War can be viewed renders every attempt inevitably incomplete and most likely biased, for the period is a sensitive one, and formative in modern China's understanding of its place in the world.[6] Of course, from Anne Noble's point of view, convoluted arguments over tariffs, taxes, duties, and measurage, not to mention the arcane jargon of the Canton trade—it was a world of *hoppos*, *chinchais*, *hongs*, *taipans*, *chumpeins* and the rest—were as impenetrable as the world of options, futures, and derivatives is to most people today. From what we know of Anne's personality, if she ever reflected on the opium trade she would—like many of her countrymen—most likely have considered it a great sin that merchants from a supposedly Christian nation could traffick in a stupefying drug—it is essentially heroin, after all—with little or no thought for the misery they were causing.

The British had begun trading directly with the Chinese in earnest at the start of the 1700s, buying and selling goods in coastal trading settlements known as 'factories' (after the merchant 'factors' who lived and worked there). From the 1750s, though, the British like all foreign merchants found themselves confined by imperial edict to a stretch of waterfront outside the southerly port city of Canton.

In those early decades of Anglo-Chinese trade, demand for each other's goods had been decidedly one-sided: the British public were thirsty for China's tea, but the Chinese were little interested in the woven broadcloth and the clockwork knick-knacks that Britain had to offer. The result of this mismatch had been a constant need for British merchants to part with silver, the precious metal with which the Chinese wished to be paid for their teas, porcelains, and silks. The fact that foreign trade was only permitted during the unhealthy tropical summer, in rather cramped factories from which wives and daughters were excluded, made things worse. It was not that these residences were inherently unpleasant; far from it: they were built of brick and granite, fitted with blinds and verandahs, and furnished much like a gentleman's club in London, with billiard rooms, libraries and dining rooms, and they were far better suited to Western ideas of comfort than even the very richest residences of Canton's mandarins. But when hundreds of men lived imprisoned within those few acres for months on end their attractions faded. They were, one resident commented, little better than 'a commercial leper colony'. Worse though than even these privations was the requirement that all foreigners deal only with a small number of local merchant guilds, the *hongs*, with all the unpredictability and arbitrary exactions that this monopoly engendered. The *hongs* kept a close eye on the Westerners, whose only avenue of legal appeal was through those very same men about whose abuses they wished to complain. Chinese were forbidden on pain of death from teaching their language to outsiders, making the commercial stranglehold of the *hongs* all the more asphyxiating. And for the world's foremost industrialized nation to be running an enormous trade deficit with agrarian China was not just an insult to British pride but a drain on the exchequer.

As the years went by, though, British merchants discovered that there was one particular commodity for which the Chinese would willingly hand over vast sums in silver. Opium might have made trading with them straightforward, too, were it not for the uncomfortable fact that it had long been prohibited in China for perfectly good reasons: as it sapped the mind and body it destroyed the lives of upright fathers and sons and was the ruin of their families. In short, its effects on the individual undermined the Confucian social structure on which China was built.

The opium poppy was well suited to the climate of British-administered Bengal, where it was grown and sold under the East India Company's monopoly. Once the white petals of the ripening seed-capsules had fallen, and once the capsule had taken on its fine, translucent coating and become a little firmer to the touch, then it was time for the lancers to walk through the poppy fields. The skin of every capsule would be lacerated to just the right depth with a *nashtar*, a concave knife made of four sharp, parallel blades, each blade held just one thirtieth of an inch from its neighbour by a cotton thread. The wounds would soon release a milky-white sap that turned to a brown gum that was laboriously scraped off, dried in the sun, and processed into cakes of opium, perfect spheres six inches in diameter and four pounds in weight. Packed forty at a time into mango-wood chests, these cakes were shipped down the Hooghly River to Calcutta to be auctioned by the British East India Company, the *de facto* government of vast swathes of northeastern India. Once the opium had been bought by private dealers, the East India Company could wash its hands of any further dealings with the drug. Whatever happened to it once it had been auctioned was, the Company insisted, none of its concern, and by this sleight of hand it could evade Chinese accusations that it was breaking Chinese law and contravening the agreements under which it traded in Canton.

When the opium arrived off the coast of China it was sold to local smugglers who undertook the illegal act of landing and selling it on. For them the punishments if caught were harsh –100 lashes and two months of wearing a heavy wooden collar for buying or smoking the drug, and summary strangulation for peddling it—but the British were quite able to stand aloof from such risks.[7] The silver which had paid for their opium found its way to the East India Company's offices in Canton to be exchanged for IOUs that could be cashed with clean hands at the East India Company's offices in London. The same silver, meanwhile, was used in Canton to buy the tea which, when landed in English ports, provided Her Majesty's Treasury with substantial sums in import duty. This was, in effect, money laundering, but of course the East India Company, the British merchants, and Whitehall could always make a convincing argument that it was somebody else, and not they themselves, who had actually broken Chinese law. Whitehall's position was that Peking had the right to ban the import of opium just like any other item of trade, but responsibility for enforcing a ban must be Peking's alone. The French (so it was pointed out by way of analogy) could ban the import of British products through Calais, but Whitehall would not be obliged to enforce that ban on Britons who wished to break French law. Unofficially, of course, Whitehall had no interest in shooting itself in the foot by enforcing China's ban on opium. Politicians and merchants would try time and again to persuade Peking to re-legalize opium, for at least this would allow the emperor to profit from its sale, but the emperor would not sacrifice his moral principles or accept advice from foreign drug-dealers. The obvious fact that the opium ban was being sidestepped by merchants and mandarins alike—a blind eye was turned by corruptible Chinese officials—played into the hands of those Britons who argued that the Chinese were hypocrites.

In the midst of such mutual suspicion and antagonism, Britain's superintendent of trade in Canton, Captain Charles Elliot, found himself in the unenviable position of defending his countrymen's commercial and legal interests in China while at the same time insisting to the Chinese that he had no authority to stop them importing opium. From a Chinese perspective, of course, this was incomprehensible: these were British merchants—how could it *not* be within Elliot's power to restrain them? Angered by such sophistry, the Chinese would regularly suspend trade in Canton to try to force Captain Elliot's hand, whereupon the opium merchants would make a temporary withdrawal and keep their heads down until the emperor was informed that the problem had abated and trade was reopened.

And so, as the decades passed, the British public slowly became addicted to China's tea, the Chinese became addicted to Britain's Bengali opium, and the Treasury became addicted to the revenue that the China trade was generating. Eventually, matters had to come to a head.

In June of 1839, while James and Anne were in England preparing the *Kite* for her next trading voyage to the Indian Ocean, an upstanding Chinese official finally achieved what others before him had not: under Commissioner Lin Zexu's supervision, 20,000 chests of opium surrendered to him by British merchants were emptied into huge pits of quicklime and sluiced out into the South China Sea. Captain Elliot himself had overseen the surrender of the drug and had promised its owners that Her Majesty's Government would indemnify them to its full value—some £2,000,000 at the time, or hundreds of millions of pounds in today's terms. But when word of the events in China reached Whitehall some four months later, the government had begged to differ: Elliot had had no authority to promise any such compensation; the *Chinese* had destroyed the merchants' opium, and the *Chinese* would pay. In January of 1840, war was declared upon the Qing dynasty. Captain Elliot and his namesake Admiral Sir George Elliot—they were in fact first cousins—were appointed by the foreign secretary Lord Palmerston to act as his plenipotentiaries in China. Their instructions were simple: with a war-fleet assembling in the Indian Ocean at their disposal, they were to capture and hold the strategically placed island of Chusan before sailing for North China. There they were to demand compensation for the destroyed opium, improved trading conditions in Canton, and access to Shanghai and other ports.

Dinghai harbour on July 4th, 1840, the eve of the British attack
(watercolour by Dr Edward Hodges Cree, © Henrietta Heawood).

3

'alas for earthly prospects'

A ND SO the *Kite*, when she dropped anchor at Madras
in April of 1840, was requisitioned as a transport ship.
She sailed first to the port of Trincomalee to load up with
stores, and there James and Anne met Dr Edward Cree,
the assistant surgeon of HMS *Rattlesnake*, who was also
bound for China with the British expedition. In his illustrated journal, Edward would later describe Anne as 'a
raw-boned, red-headed Scotchwoman'—why he thought
she was Scottish is a mystery, however, given that she must
have spoken with a Wiltshire accent, while her husband
James had spent his formative years in London.

The *Kite's* final anchorage before China was at the island
of Singapore, which was by then a wholly British possession
and the capital of the Straits Settlement. John Lee Scott,
our nineteen-year-old apprentice mariner, recorded what
happened next:

> Whilst we lay at Singapore, the *Melville*, *Blonde*, and
> *Pylades* arrived, and we received orders to sail for
> Macao immediately, at which place we arrived after a
> short passage, but were still behind the fleet, it having
> sailed some days before for Chusan. We received
> orders to follow it to Buffalo Island, where there was
> to be a man of war cruising to give us farther direc-
> tions; but when we arrived at this island we found no
> vessel of any kind; and as we had had a very quick
> passage, Mr. Noble was afraid to proceed any further,

as perhaps we might have passed the fleet, and
arrived before it. We therefore brought the ship to an
anchor, and lay there till the next afternoon, when the
Melville and a transport arrived, upon which we got
under weigh, and followed the *Melville* up to Chusan,
where we arrived the day following, and anchored in
the outer roads. We found the town in the possession
of our own troops, who had taken it the day previous
to our arrival: so that if we had not stopped at Buffalo
Island, we should have been present at the attack; we
heard the firing, and saw the blaze of the burning
town whilst on our passage up.

The 'burning town' was in fact the harbour district of
the walled city of Dinghai, which lay a mile inland. The
previous afternoon, July 5th, the warship HMS *Wellesley*
had led a short but ferocious naval bombardment of the
local garrison's makeshift defences. Three regiments of
British troops and several more of native Indian sepoys had
landed unopposed, discovered great quantities of a strong
spirit called *samshu*, and drunkenly set about looting and
burning homes, warehouses, and temples. Early on the
morning of July 6th, before the *Kite* had dropped anchor,
British soldiers had marched through the gates of Dinghai
and raised a flag of conquest. Scott witnessed the aftermath
of the fighting:

> The men-of-war junks which had fired on the
> *Wellesley* presented a most wretched appearance,
> being deserted — some sunk, and others with their
> masts shot away; and where a shot had struck the
> hull, it had not only passed completely through the
> vessel, but also through one or two houses ashore.
> There were not many Chinese to be seen, and the
> few that were still in the town, appeared of the very

lowest grade. The town and harbour presented, nevertheless, rather a lively spectacle, as boats were constantly passing between the ships and the shore, disembarking troops of varied dress and nations. Two camps were very soon formed, one overlooking the town, and the other on a hill commanding the entrance into the harbour.

'Sickness,' Scott noted with considerable understatement, 'soon began to make its appearance amongst the troops.' The army's provisioning for the arrival on Chusan at the height of summer of 3,500 infantry and artillerymen, not to mention their servants and camp-followers, had been poor, and the results were as predictable as they were regrettable. Much of the salt meat packed in India had gone bad and many troops went hungry; men baked in canvas bell-tents carelessly pitched amongst malarial paddyfields; typhus and cholera broke out. Worst of all, by drinking bad water pumped from field-ditches, the majority of the invading forces contracted severe dysentery. Soon there were only 800 men well enough to attend roll-call, and even these, in the opinion of one naval surgeon, could best be likened to 'animated corpses'.[1] Some of the Hindu troops were all but starving to death, too ill to cook but incapable of eating anything prepared by a man of inferior caste. The lack of fresh food had got so bad that the symptoms of scurvy had begun to show. 'Graves are forever open,' a sergeant of the Cameronian Regiment lamented, 'and those who assist in paying the last duties to their ill-fated companions look as if they would soon follow.'[2] 'I would rather spend five years in Bengal even on half *batta*† than as many months in this most accursed place,' wrote another.[3]

---

† An extra allowance paid to an officer for serving in India.

The *Kite* lay at anchor in Dinghai harbour for a few weeks, during which her stores were unloaded and replaced by half a dozen 'carronades'—short cannons that could be used at sea with little training—besides four 32-pounder naval guns, a large cache of captured Chinese ordnance, and fourteen massive two-ton barrels of water by way of ballast. James Noble was given the temporary rank of 'second master' in the Royal Navy and was replaced in overall command by Charles Henry Douglas, a 25-year-old lieutenant from HMS *Wellesley* who had entered the navy as a midshipman at the tender age of twelve.

In all, the *Kite* was by now home to thirty-five souls: under Lieutenant Douglas were Captain Noble, along with his wife and baby son, and the 29-year-old chief officer, Mr Richard Goldsmith Witts. As well as John Lee Scott, there were three other apprentice mariners—Pellew Webb (who at nineteen was the same age as Scott), acting second mate Henry Twizell (who was eighteen), and another young lad named William Wombwell. Webb and Twizell had never even worked aboard any other vessel, both having been apprenticed to the *Kite* in Newcastle before she had ever gone to sea.[4] There was also another Englishman whose name we do not discover in Scott's *Narrative*, an Italian, a Filipino, ten Indian lascar sailors, and the ship's Bengali cook. Lieutenant Douglas also brought with him seven Royal Marines and five 'first-class ship's boys' from HMS *Melville*, who, Scott recalled, were not actually boys but instead experienced sailors, 'all above one-and-twenty'.

On August 1st, 1840, Charles and George Elliot left Chusan aboard HMS *Wellesley*, bound for the mouth of the Peiho river some 800 miles to the north (for this was the closest a warship could get to the Chinese capital) to negotiate terms with the emperor's representatives. Not long after the *Wellesley* had departed, Lieutenant

Douglas hoisted his pennant over the *Kite* and she sailed
with dispatches for a small flotilla that was surveying the
estuary of the Yangtze River. The importance of accurately
mapping what were still largely uncharted waters was
driven home when the *Kite* grounded on a sandbank there
for several days, during which time one Royal Marine and
one of the ship's boys died of dysentery. On September
12th the *Kite* was helped off the sandbank by one of the
survey vessels and, since she lay too low in the water to be
of use in the shallow river, Captain Noble plotted a course
back to Dinghai and the safety of the British fleet. But the
Kite never made it home. John Lee Scott recorded what
happened:

> We brought up that night, and got under weigh next
> afternoon; anchored again at dusk, and very unfor-
> tunately, just before daybreak, our jolly-boat broke
> adrift, and was carried away by the tide. The gig was
> manned, and sent after her, and we followed in the
> vessel, as soon as we could get our anchor: we picked
> up both boats, but not without a great deal of trouble;
> the gig we hoisted up on the starboard quarter, and
> the jolly-boat was towed astern.

The 'jolly-boat' was the smallest of the rowing boats carried
by a ship such as the *Kite*, and it was used to perform all
the everyday tasks that required crewmen to leave the ship.
Around 5 or 6 yards long, it was lowered and raised on
ropes and hung from davits at the stern of the ship when
not in use. Since Scott records that it 'broke adrift', it was
most likely being towed behind the *Kite* at the end of a
rope which now failed. The 'gig', for ferrying the captain
to and from shore, would have been larger than the jolly.
The 'starboard quarter' was the right-hand side of the

ship, toward the stern, which was the normal position for storing the gig when it was not being used.

> We anchored again at night, and next morning started with a fine fair wind, expecting to be at Chusan in a day or two. At this time all the marines but one, two of the first-class boys, and Webb and Wombwell, were ill of the dysentery, leaving very few hands to work the ship.

This final anchorage, so we learn from Lieutenant Douglas' account of that day in the *Singapore Free Press*, had been amongst the northernmost scattered islets of the Chusan archipelago. The rescuing of the jolly-boat had wasted a great deal of time, and by day's end the *Kite* was only around 20 miles closer to Chusan and the safety of Dinghai harbour and the British flotilla. The following morning, at 4.30am, the anchor had been raised and the *Kite* had steered for the southwest, Captain Noble no doubt wishing to keep to deeper water to avoid the shallows and the unpredictable tidal races to be encountered around the larger islands. Such a course, though, placed the *Kite*'s fate in the hands of the immensely powerful tides of Hangzhou Bay, where twice daily the waters of the East China Sea are sucked into a narrow bottleneck.

At twenty minutes before noon, the *Kite* having been underway for some seven hours and having made considerable ground, Lieutenant Douglas came up on deck and suggested to Captain Noble that 'a pull of the weather brace would do no harm'. Douglas later recalled what happened next:

> Captain Noble immediately turned round to the helmsman and discovered that he had suffered the ship to fall off considerably from her course, which

was west-by-southwest. A cast of the lead gave only
2½ fathoms, a second two fathoms, and a third in a
quick succession only a few feet. On the water first
shoaling the anchor was instantly let go; but such was
the furious state of the tide (running at the rate of 7 or
8 knots) [around 9 mph] that upwards of 30 fathoms
were run out without having the slightest effect in
bringing the vessel up. Eventually she brought herself
up by striking on the edge of a quick sand, and while
in this position, commenced bumping most violently,
and swinging round with such rapidity that Lieut.
Douglas expected every instant to see the topmasts
jerked out of her. A few moments' continuance of
this motion embedded the vessel firmly in the sand,
broadside on to the tide, and remaining steady but for
an instant she commenced to heel over gradually, and
finally lay right over on her broadside with her lower
masts in the water. It now became evident the vessel
was irrecoverably lost, and nothing remained but to
use every exertion for the preservation of life.[5]

John Lee Scott had been below decks looking after Webb
and Wombwell, both ill with dysentery, when Captain
Noble realized the danger the ship was in and ordered the
anchor be let go:

I immediately jumped on deck, ran forward, and let
go the stopper; the vessel was now striking heavily
aft, all the chain on deck (about sixty fathoms) ran
out with so much velocity that the windlass caught
fire. The vessel being by the stern, and catching the
ground there, the anchor holding her forward, she
could not get end on to the tide, and was conse-
quently broadside on, and as it was running like a
sluice, she was capsized in a moment.

The rising tide had carried the *Kite* far to the west of where she was meant to be, and instead of finding five fathoms of water beneath her she had run aground some two miles from the shore, on the vast, muddy shoals of Hangzhou Bay. Where precisely is unclear, but the *Singapore Free Press* provides us with some good clues:

> The exact position of the *Kite* was not known at the time she struck, as that happened shortly before noon; but as far as he had the means of judging, Lieut. Douglas believes it to be about 35 [miles] from Chunghae, then bearing from the vessel southwest.

Chunghae is a common misspelling of Zhenhai, the name of the fortified town that commanded the mouth of the largest river on that part of the coast; 'southwest' is a little more confusing, since such a position would have put the *Kite* in open waters far from the shore. But if we assume that either Douglas or the typesetter of the *Free Press* was mistaken and the correct bearing for Zhenhai was in fact south*east*, then 35 miles would put the *Kite* in exactly the same location as the reports written by the local mandarins at the time. These mention two particular embankments—the Lijitang (meaning 'profitable levee') and the longer Niniutang ('muddy ox levee'). As the Qiantang River deposited its silt, the local farmers had for centuries been reclaiming land from the sea, and levees defined each new stretch of solid ground in much the same way as a tree's rings mark the laying down of new wood. Both levees survive to this day, and so we can say with a fair degree of certainty that the *Kite* ran aground on the sandbanks that lay to the northeast of the present-day town of Fuhai. Today, though, that same spot lies some two or three miles inland, lost beneath a network of fields and irrigation canals. But while those contemporary Chinese accounts can help us to pinpoint where the *Kite* went down, they paint a completely different picture from those of Anne Noble, John Lee Scott, and Lieutenant Douglas in other matters. When the *Kite* was spotted, they record,

> Yuyao's district magistrate Wang Zhongyang met with his assistant Sun Yingzhao, deputy Li Ningyu from Sanshan, Sergeant Ma Jinlong of the city garrison, Corporal Shen Zhen of the Xushan guardpost, and others, to raise the defences in the area around the Lijitang levee. Wang Zhongyang ordered two patrols to go to sea to scout out the situation. Because there was nothing but quicksand beyond the levee, foreign ships with their deep draught would be sure to get stuck if they ventured into the shallows; and so he also ordered that if the patrols encountered a foreign ship they should create some ruse to draw it close to the levee, where it could more easily be attacked. That evening, a foreign ship approached the coast from the direction of Cixi and, observing that our patrol boats carried only a few soldiers, gave chase. But when the patrols headed for the levee to get away, the foreigners, unfamiliar with the lie of the land, chased them right onto the sands and got stuck.

Given that Anne, Scott, and Douglas all agree that the *Kite* ran aground because her helmsman had failed to maintain the course for Dinghai in the teeth of a swiftly rising tide, any claims by local mandarins that they deliberately lured her to her doom are best dismissed as wishful thinking or self-aggrandisement.

Everybody who had been on deck when the *Kite* struck bottom was either thrown into the open water or left clinging to the wreck. John Lee Scott and Henry Twizell had survived being swept away by holding tight to the

Survivors clinging to the wreck of the *Kite*, as pictured in John
Lee Scott's *Narrative*. The rowing boat with Anne, Mr Witts, and
Lieutenant Douglas aboard can be seen in the background.

mainmast and its shrouds. Below decks, most of the crew
had been lying in their hammocks suffering from dysentery,
the greater part of them practically naked; miraculously,
none had drowned, and Scott helped them onto the ship's
side as they emerged from the hatchways. The *Singapore
Free Press* explained how Anne had only barely escaped
with her life:

> Lieutenant Douglas was at this moment supporting
> himself by the top of the companion, when he heard
> some one screaming in the water, and recognised the
> voice to be that of Mrs Noble, the Captain's wife. ...
> He jumped into the water, and found Mrs Noble, who
> had been thrown overboard by the heel of the vessel,
> nearly exhausted, but holding on under the bulwark
> by a small iron knee which supported the quarter
> davit.† In hopes of saving the lady, and then if possible

---

† A crane-like structure on which the ship's boats were raised.

56

hauling alongside the main mast to give such directions as he thought necessary, Lieutenant Douglas reached the [jolly] boat, and, with the assistance of Mr Witts, the chief officer, succeeded in getting Mrs Noble into it. An attempt was then made to reach the main mast, but as the boat (at this time full of water and in a sinking state) was bound by the tide to an impenetrable mass of cordage, sails, etc., the effort was fruitless, and the only chance left was to cut their way through.

Scott threw them a knife, and with this they cut a path through the tangled rigging and were carried away by the current. Not four minutes had passed since the *Kite* had first run aground, and no testimony of the devastating effect of those few minutes could be more powerful than Anne's. Noting that they had hoped to reach Chusan in two days, true to her trust in God's Providence rather than in human plans she then observed that: 'Alas for earthly prospects; they are indeed fallacious.'

About twelve o'clock in the forenoon, the vessel struck on an awful quicksand, not laid down in the chart. The shock was as sudden as it was dreadful; all efforts at the moment were used, but in vain, and in a few moments, almost before we could think or speak, or alas! even have time to fetch my sweet child from the cabin, the vessel went over with a tremendous crash on her broadside, and every creature on board (except my dear child) was precipitated with great violence into the sea. The moment was so dreadful I saw nothing, and, whether my beloved husband, who was giving orders till the last moment, ran to the cabin to save his darling child, or whether he fell with the rest, I know not; but alas! he was never seen or heard of more; his last words to me were 'hold on, Anne'!

never, never shall I forget them. My sweet child must have perished in his cradle. I tremble to think of the sufferings of them both. Oh! how often have I wished I had shared the same grave, yet the will of God was otherwise, and I know it is very wicked, but when you know my almost unparalleled sufferings you will not wonder at it.

Anne would spend the next eight days in the forlorn hope that James and Ralph might somehow have survived. But as John Lee Scott was to learn from the two boys who were in the cabin when the *Kite* heeled over, everything had fallen to the starboard side where Ralph was sleeping, and they had escaped through the skylight, 'leaving the poor baby to its fate'. It's likely that Ralph's cot was a makeshift affair, fastened to the hull to prevent it from tumbling about in rough seas, and he might even have been sown into his bedding for safety. Even his own mother or father might have been powerless to save him. 'To return to the wreck,' Anne's account continues,

after struggling under water for some time, I caught hold of one of the iron bars that held the boat on the quarter, to which I clung, my body being still in the water, and the breakers coming over me with great force. A poor little dog saved itself on my breast for some time, but at last I was obliged to put it off; oh! had it been my darling child, I would have died rather a thousand times. Lieut. Douglas arose close by me, and although for a time he could not help me, yet I shall ever remember with the deepest gratitude the kind manner in which he stood by me, doing all in his power to soothe me, and, by his orders, to save the lives of all. Oh! could I picture to you the scene at this moment—the vessel on her broadside, her masts and sails in the water, numbers of persons rising and, clinging to the wreck, the horror of every countenance, and the dreadful noise of the breakers, but it is too much even to tell you I saw it all; never, never shall I forget the sight. Lieut. Douglas, with Mr. Witts the chief officer, who now kindly came forward to my aid, did all in their power to save me, and they were, by the blessing of God, the means of preserving my unhappy life. These two gentlemen, with the poor cabin boys,[†] got into the boat. I had just strength to raise my foot, of which one of the gentlemen took hold, drew the boat to, and lifted me in. The boat being nearly full of water, and the breakers still coming over it every moment, the gentlemen were obliged to cut the rope to prevent her sinking. The current immediately took her, and nothing could prevent her from leaving the wreck. The people had now got on the upper side of the vessel. I strained my eyes in vain to find those so dear to me. I saw all but them. I tore my hair in despair and called till they could hear me no longer, telling them to seek my husband and child. Hour after hour the wreck was seen; at last we lost sight of it entirely.

Of course, Anne herself would have been clinging to the wreck with the other survivors had it not been for Lieutenant Douglas. As it was, she had no idea whether James and Ralph were amongst them or not.

You will fancy me weeping and screaming all this time; I assure you, *no*: my trouble was *too* overwhelming; I could not shed a tear, although my heart was fit to break; I sat more like a statue, my eyes seeking in vain for the wreck. The boat's little kedger was thrown out,

† Despite the rather disparaging term used to describe them, these two lascar 'cabin boys' would have been fully grown men.

and the water rushing by was almost like a wall on either side of our boat. We saw many things washed from the wreck pass us. About 4 o'clock the current turned in our favour, and after some hours of anxiety we came in sight of the wreck; as we drew near, we found the vessel had sunk in the sand and only her maintop was now in sight, to which all the poor sufferers clung for life. Efforts were made to reach the wreck, but it was impossible. Lieut. Douglas spoke to the men and told them to make a raft, hoping on the morrow to be able to render them some assistance. We now again left the wreck and night began to set in; the gentlemen lay down in the bottom of the boat, and I sat and kept watch by the stars. It was a beautiful moonlight night, but I need not say it appeared very long, and often did I speak to Lieut. Douglas who slept very little.

On the 16th, we again passed the wreck early, and, as before, strove in vain to reach the poor crew. A few words were spoken, until we were carried away by the current. In the afternoon we passed the wreck for the last time; everything possible was done to reach it but to no purpose; and after speaking a few words, once more we had to endure the trial of being carried past.

Anne can be forgiven for misremembering the sequence of events: John Lee Scott and the other survivors had in fact left the wreck on the 15th. Her account goes on:

What our feelings were, none but those in a like situation can conceive. It was now again night, and, as before, I kept my melancholy watch. After this we could not find the wreck, and we were obliged to come to the dreadful conclusion, that all the crew must have perished, or have been taken from the wreck by the Chinese. I now felt almost sure that

I was a widow, and all alone in the world; but yet I think I hoped even against hope, and Lieut. Douglas, who was most kind to me, rather led me to believe such happiness possible. Oh! could I only tell you all of the kindness I received from that dear gentleman. One remark he made, when I felt almost heart broken, was, 'depend on it, my dear Mrs. Noble, the Almighty has preserved you for a future and a better purpose.' Thus did he at all times, in the most kind and soothing manner, try to cheer my truly sad heart. Picture for a moment our situation—five of us in a small boat: with little clothing—the gentlemen being but thinly clad, and myself in a thin morning gown, no bonnet, no shawl, and no shoes, the latter having been washed off: no food, no water, no sail, only two oars and near an enemy's country.

On this day, we went on board a fishing boat; the men were kind to us and gave us a little dry rice, some water, and an old mat to try to make a sail of. Soon after, we thought we saw a small English sail; never shall I forget the excitement we felt; but after a long time, we found we were mistaken. Towards evening we picked up a small pumpkin, of which I took a little—the first food I had taken since the wreck. Whilst we were thus driven about from place to place, again we thought we saw a steamer, and we did all in our power to make them observe us, raising a signal of distress on one of our oars, and once more we were as before disappointed.

On Wednesday night the breakers came over our little boat, with such violence, that we thought she would have sunk; it washed away one of our oars, and we were all wet through; but still the Almighty preserved us, glory be to his holy name! Lieutenant Douglas and myself had a prayer together, in which we thanked God, for all his past mercies, and asked his future protection; we were very cold but felt comforted.

Anne's boat had by now drifted back and forth with the current until it was some forty or fifty miles from the wreck. When dawn broke the next day, it was found that the flood tide had swept them some way up a narrow tributary of the Qiantang River—most likely the Cao'e River—but then the ebb tide carried them back to the Qiantang. There, in desperate need of fresh water, they boarded a junk, promising the crew $20 if they would take them to Chusan. Towing the jolly-boat behind it, this junk entered a creek—there are many on this stretch of coast—but within three miles it had grounded on the next ebb tide and its master had changed his mind about having these five foreigners aboard. Given a small supply of water, they were once more compelled to take to their boat. The next flood tide swept them along, but far from taking them closer to safety the creek instead became narrower at every turn until eventually the boat became stuck beside what both Douglas and Anne both describe as 'a bank'—probably one of the levees that protect the farmland from inundation—from where they could plainly see the gates of 'a large city'. Its location is a bit of a mystery: there were no cities in the vicinity, and the only settlement of any size was Lihai. But surrounded as it then was by high, gated walls some 600 yards long on each side, and augmented with watchtowers and pavilions, Lihai would have struck any English eyewitness as a city rather than the small garrison town it in fact was.[6]

'It now began to rain a little,' Anne was later to recall, 'and at night we found ourselves in a small creek, with numbers of Chinamen round us. They appeared kind and brought us a little boiled rice.'

Wonderful to say, although we had been so long without food, not one in the boat complained of hunger, and of the rice now brought very little was eaten; the rain now fell fast, and we all lay down in the bottom of the boat, and laid the old mat over the top. About 12 o'clock, I thought I heard foot steps, and on looking up saw about twenty Chinamen round our boat, carrying gay lanterns. I awoke Lieut. Douglas in alarm; however, they still appeared kind and gave us more food. In the morning, it being very wet, we went barefooted to a Chinaman's house. After sitting a short time, they told us, that they would get us something to eat, and then take us to Chusan. We followed; they took us to a temple for shelter from the rain. One of the party now left us, and we began to suspect that all was not right, and set off to regain our boat.

We cannot say for sure who precisely led this party of Chinese, but the City Annals of Ningbo record that on this day 'a salt-maker named Hu Chengjin took five British people prisoner'.[7] Anne and the others very soon realised the position they were in: 'Alas! it was too late.'

We had scarcely ascended the bank, when, on looking behind, we saw a large party of soldiers, a Mandarin, and numbers of Chinese, pursuing us. We saw at once we were betrayed; flight was impossible, resistance as vain. I was leaning on Lieut. Douglas's arm; he stood boldly in my defence, but it was of no use, for they struck me several times. They then put chains around our necks, hurrying us along a path, not half a yard in breadth, to a large city, through every street of which they led us. The people thronged by thousands to stare, so that we could scarcely pass. Their savage cries were terrific. From this they led us to a temple full of soldiers, and one of the wretches stole my wedding ring from my finger, the only thing I treasured. Alas! that I was not to keep that one dear pledge of my husband's affection. They then set a table and wrote Chinese, asking if we understood it. Never shall I forget that temple, their fierce grimaces and savage threats. Hitherto Lieut. Douglas had been my only friend, and, I think I may say, that we have been a mutual comfort to one another throughout our sufferings. But we were now to part. The soldiers bound Lieut. Douglas's hands behind him and tied him to a post, and in this situation I was forced from him. We took an affectionate leave of one another, as friends never expecting to meet again, until we met in heaven. He gave me his black silk handkerchief to tie round my waist, which I shall ever treasure as a remembrance of that truly sad moment. We antici-pated instant death in its most cruel form, and I think, I could say surely the bitterness of death is past. I now felt indeed alone.

Mr. Witts, one of the boys, and myself were now again dragged through the rain, and my feet being bare slipped at every step, and they were at last obliged to bring me a pair of straw sandals. I was obliged to hang to the coat of a tall man, who held me by the chain. We must have looked wretched in the extreme, our clothes being much covered with dirt as well as drenched with rain. My hair hung disheveled round my neck.

Anne's concern for her appearance points to an aspect of her ordeal which would have far less resonance today: as a respectable married woman she would have worn her hair up, and tightly dressed, and she would have felt immensely vulnerable to be seen with it hanging loose. Nor is her earlier reference to her clothing—'a thin morning gown,

One of the prisoners being led in chains (from Scott's *Narrative*).

no bonnet, no shawl, and no shoes'—merely given as incidental detail: she would normally have worn a bonnet and shawl when outdoors and would have been keenly aware of their absence; a 'morning gown' was the usual wear for a woman when indoors at home in the early part of the day. It would have consisted of an easy-fitting, long-sleeved, white gown made from cotton or a lightweight 'lawn' fabric, would sometimes be worn with a matching cap, was sometimes trimmed with ruffles, and sometimes embroidered in white thread. Dressed in such a gown, Anne must also have been wearing the appropriate under-clothing—a chemise next to her skin, then over this a corset, and also a light cotton petticoat.[8] It was far from suitable attire for a lengthy trek in the pouring rain.

> In this state we must have walked at least 20 miles, and passed through numberless cities, all the inhabitants of which crowded around us; their hooting and savage yells were frightful. We twice passed through water nearly up to our waist. After having reached a

temple, we were allowed to rest ourselves on some stones. They gave us here some prison clothes and food. At night they laid down some mats and a quilt, on either side of a large temple.

Once again, Anne's recollections, terrified and grief-stricken as she was, are hard to square with what we know of the geography of this corner of China: rather than 'numberless cities', there were only villages and two or three small towns anywhere near, though they would have been very densely inhabited. We can be confident, though, that it was in Yuyao, upriver from Ningbo, that they were soon to be put onto boats, and so this temple in which she rested must have been in or near a city named Shangyu.

Mr. Witts and the boy took one side, and after a short prayer to my almighty, heavenly father, I lay down but not to sleep; the chain round our necks being fastened to the wall. Would that I could describe to you the scene: the temple beautifully lighted up with lanterns, our miserable beds and more miserable selves, all the dark faces of the frightful looking Chinese, (of whom I think there were eight,) the smoke from their long pipes, the din of the gongs and other noises which they kept up all night were indeed horrid. Long, very long, did this night appear.

It was an ancient practice throughout China for night-watchmen to show they were alert by keeping up a continuous, loud rapping on bamboo tubes, a noise which all the prisoners found made sleeping difficult if not impossible.

Morning at last dawned, and the keepers brought us a little water to wash with, which was a great comfort; after which they led us to an open court, to be exposed to the public gaze of numberless spectators to come throughout the day. Here they took our height, the length of our hair, and noted every feature in an exact manner, and then made us write an account of the wreck of the *Kite*. In the evening I was taken to see the Mandarin's wife and daughters, but although my appearance must have been wretched in the extreme, they did not evince the least feeling towards me, but rather treated me as an object of scorn. This I felt the more, as I was enabled to make them understand, that I had lost both my dear husband and child in the wreck. We remained here two days and three nights, derided and taunted by all around us.

On the morning of Monday the 21st they took the end of our chains, and bade us follow them. They put our coats and quilts into small cages, just such as we should think a proper place to confine a wild beast in; mine was scarcely a yard high, a little more than ¾ of a yard long, and a little more than half a yard broad. The door opened from the top. Into these we were lifted, the chain round our necks being locked to the cover. They put a long piece of bamboo through the middle, a man took either end, and in this manner we were jolted from city to city,† to suffer insults from the rabble, the cries of whom were awful; but my God had not forsaken me, and even then, although a widow and in the hands of such bitter enemies, and expecting death at every moment, I could remember with delight, that Christ my Saviour had said—'I am the resurrection and the life, he that believeth on me, though he were dead, yet shall he live'; and through the blessing of the Almighty, I was enabled to sing praises to God aloud. I need not tell you, my dear and

† Again, their journey would in fact have taken them through two or three small towns.

much loved friend, how much I thought of my sweet and once happy home, and my dear fatherless child, and how fervently I prayed to that God of mercy and goodness, who had so wonderfully upheld me in all my sufferings, to bless her also. Death was nothing to me: I longed to be with my Saviour to praise him for ever, and to meet again my affectionate husband and sweet child, who were more than life to me. Oh my dear friend! how often do my feelings at this and many other times of my suffering shame me, when I feel myself cold in my duty towards my Redeemer. In my body I was now very weak, having scarcely eaten any thing since the wreck, but my spirit was strong in the Lord.

At this point, Anne reached the walled city of Yuyao, which sits on its eponymous river some forty miles upstream from Ningbo. Between the two cities runs a long, flat river-valley four miles broad, bounded on both sides by low mountains that form an ever-present feature. Today the river is over 300 metres wide in places, but it was even wider in the 1840s. Anne describes it as 'a canal', possibly because its upper reaches had weirs built to keep the water deep and navigable.

> We again stopped at another city and were taken out of our cages, having heavy irons put on our legs, with a chain half a yard long. Mr. Witts and the boy had also irons on their wrists; although I saw mine, they did not put them on at that time. The former were carried on board one boat, and I myself put into another, and thus we proceeded two days and three nights on a canal, during which time I did not taste any food, as they would not permit me to get out of my little cage on any account. You may judge what my sufferings were.

I believe it was Wednesday the 23d. that we arrived at Ningpo. You may imagine my happiness in finding my friend Lieut. Douglas, and my delight to hear that he had been treated rather better than myself, and had arrived here a short time before. I also heard with gratitude and joy, that all the *Kite*'s crew had been taken from the wreck by the Chinese and were prisoners in the city. But alas, alas! with all this good news my worst fears were confirmed, that all I treasured lay buried in the ocean. What can I say—my dear child could not have lived in an open boat and suffered as I had done, and my devoted husband, being of a warm and most affectionate temper would not, could not, have lived to have seen me suffer as I have suffered, and how would it have torn my heart to have seen those, ten thousand times dearer to me than my own life, endure so much! I humbly pray to be enabled to say, 'thy will be done!' God has I believe in goodness and mercy taken my treasures, who was able to do for them more than I could even ask or think. And although I am left destitute and alone and far from home, yet in his mercy he has raised you up, my truly Christian friend, with many many others for my comfort, on account of which I shall praise the Saviour both in time and eternity; and want whatever I may, may I ever possess a thankful heart.

In a letter written from her cell in Ningbo, Anne would later tell Mary Gutzlaff that her husband James was the third of his family to die at sea.[9]

'Mrs Noble on her way to Ningpo' (by Edward Cree, © Henrietta Heawood).

4

'a most unenviable state'

B UT James had been exceptionally unfortunate, and was in fact the only adult to have been drowned in the sinking of the *Kite*. The rest—both her regular crew and also the sailors and marines seconded from the navy—had survived the initial disaster and had made it to shore more quickly than those in the jolly-boat. Had Anne stayed with the ship, she would have experienced a very different—and arguably worse—capture. Once more, the Chinese reports from the time of how the rest of the men were taken prisoner are at odds with how John Lee Scott recalled the events: 'The foreigners had deployed their guns and cannons,' it was reported to the emperor in Beijing,

> and by the morning of the 21st of the month [i.e. September 16th], with the ship was stuck ever deeper in the sand, they were scared out of their wits. Our officers led their troops, riding in small boats right up to the side of the ship's hull and jumping into her cabins, taking twenty-two of these foreign bandits captive, of whom two, badly injured, died forthwith. Some of the others leapt into a sampan and fled, while others jumped into the sea and drowned. Our troops salvaged a pair of brass cannon from the ship.

Though two cannon were indeed taken from the wreck of the *Kite*, the rest of the report seems to have been embroidered to make the local militia appear rather more daring than they were. John Lee Scott, who had watched helplessly as Anne's jolly-boat was swept away, was left marooned on the mainmast as the weight of water in the sails gradually caused the ship to break apart. With the tide rising, he and the other survivors had tried to make a serviceable raft with any wood they could salvage. They had managed to lash together a good many spars, only to find themselves surrounded by junks, two of which were full of Chinese soldiers. Happy to take their chances with the enemy rather than drown—if Scott's story is to be relied upon—they had boarded the junks and refused to leave, despite the soldiers' protests.

When Scott's junk set its sail, however, it almost immediately ran aground on the ebb tide, and he and the others were led across the mudflats by the light of a lantern to another junk that too lay waiting to be floated off. For the first time since leaving Dinghai harbour, they finally set foot on dry land in the small hours of the morning, at the Muddy Ox Levee. Scott's account of their subsequent treatment at the hands of the local farmers and militiamen is fuller than Anne's, dwelling more on the physicality of their experiences and the details of their surroundings and less on the emotions they must have gone through. He leaves us with a very immediate impression of the locals' reactions to these foreigners' sudden and unwelcome arrival, which range from acts of curiosity and genuine kindness through to hatred, violence, and even murder. The *Kite*, we must not forget, had run aground barely two months after the unprovoked bombardment of a city just forty miles away.

> The Chinese made signs to us, that if we would follow them, they would give us something to eat; we accordingly walked after them until we arrived at a small village, which consisted of a few miserable mud

huts, with but one respectable brick house; but from these few huts a swarm of men, women, and children, poured out on our approach. We were taken into an outhouse, one half of which was occupied by an immense buffalo, and in the other half was a cane bed with musquito curtains; in one corner was a ladder, leading to a loft containing another couch. They now brought us some hot rice, and a kind of preserved vegetable: we contented ourselves with the rice and a basin of tea, the preserve being so exceedingly nasty we could none of us eat it. Whilst in this place, a Chinese, who seemed the superior of the village, and doubtless was the owner of the one brick house, brought a piece of paper written upon in Chinese characters, and made signs for one of us to write upon it; intimating at the same time that he had written some account of us on this paper, and that he wanted an account in our writing, which I accordingly gave him, stating the time and cause of our shipwreck, and also our present situation; hoping that he would take it to the mandarin of the district, and that from him it might be forwarded to the authorities at Chusan, who might thus learn where we were, and take some steps for our return to the fleet.

When it was broad daylight we mentioned the name of Ningpo, and they made signs that if we would go with them they would show us the way there, so we started, as we imagined, for Ningpo. Having no trousers, and my only clothing being a flannel shirt, and a black silk handkerchief round my head, which Twizell had given me when in the maintop, they gave me a piece of matting, but this proving rather an encumbrance than of any service, I soon threw it off, and walked on *sans culottes*.

We passed in this style through a highly culti-vated country; on every side large plantations of cotton and rice, and various kinds of vegetables, but all unknown to me. Having gone six or seven miles, seeing very few houses, but crowds of people turning out of each as we passed, we at length arrived at a cross-road. Here another party of Chinese appeared, who absolutely forbade our proceeding any further: but as our guides went on, and beckoned us to follow, we pushed through our opponents and walked on; but they, having collected more men, headed us, and we were obliged to come to a stand-still. In this case we found the want of a perfect understanding amongst ourselves, for the Lascars were so frightened at their situation, that they fell on their knees before the Chinamen, which of course encouraged the latter, and before we could look around us, men rose up as it were from the ground, separated us, and made us all prisoners at once, with the exception of four, who ran off, though without any idea whither they should run, or what they should do. Here the Syrang† made a foolish attempt to cut his throat with a rusty old knife he had about him, but he only succeeded in tearing his flesh a little, for he was soon disarmed and pinioned. If, perhaps, we had all stood together, and put a bold face on the matter, though without any kind of arms, we might have gone quietly to the mandarin's, and then been treated properly, but the conduct of the Lascars emboldened our enemies, and we were seized, bound, and dragged off, almost before we knew where we were. As to those who ran away, they were obliged to give themselves up after a short run, and got a very severe beating, besides several wounds from the spears the Chinese were armed with.

† The man in charge of the ship's lascar sailors, collecting and distributing their wages, managing their affairs, and so on.

When we were seized in the manner I have related, a man threw his arms round me, and though I could easily have shaken him off, I saw five or six others gathering round me, and I thought it would be useless to struggle. It was better for me that I made no resistance, as the others were bound and dragged away, with ropes round their necks; whereas the man who first seized me, still held me, and walked me off, without binding me at all. Twizell was amongst those that ran, and I did not see him again till I got to Ningpo. As I was walking along with my keeper, we were met by two soldiers, who immediately stopped, and one, armed with a spear, prepared to make a lunge at me; but my old man stepped between us, and spoke to him, upon which he dropped his spear, and allowed us to pass.

At length we arrived at a large village, and here my first keeper left me, much to my regret, as, after he was gone, my hands, hitherto free, were made fast behind my back, and the cord being drawn as tight as possible, the flesh soon swelled and caused me great pain; another rope was put round my neck, by which they led me about.

At times I gave myself up for lost, but still I could not fancy the Chinese to be so cruel a people, as to murder us in cold blood, particularly after the manner in which we had fallen into their hands. I hardly knew what to think.

It is worthwhile pausing for a moment to consider the treatment being meted out to the prisoners. They themselves thought it harsh, and the British public would be outraged when they learned of it, but how were they being treated by the Chinese standards of the day? In actual fact, rather than being singled out, they were treated much the same as if they had been locals accused of a crime. On the face of it, these foreigners were clearly guilty of landing on Chinese soil without the permission that was required by law, and they could have expected to be taken into custody even had there not been fighting between their two nations. It was normal practice in Qing-dynasty China for arrestees to be led to gaol with a chain or a rope around the neck, to have shackles or manacles riveted on, or to be carried about in a cage. And far from being so cruel a people as to murder captives in cold blood, the Chinese were heirs to a well-developed code of penal statutes, and the mandarins to whom it had fallen to deal with these unexpected castaways were required to follow the correct procedures—duly informing their superiors of the arrests, examining and questioning their prisoners, taking statements, and looking after their basic needs. Constables or runners in the employ of the local magistrate would see to it that they were guarded and could not escape, but it is unsurprising, given that the local populace was angry and afraid at the violence being done by the British, that they carried out their duties with little regard for the comfort of their charges.

> My new keeper led me into the courtyard of a house, and made me fast to one of several pillars that supported a rude kind of verandah, dragging the rope as tight as he could; however, he brought me some water to drink, when I made signs for it. I had not been here long, when one of the *Melville*'s people[†] was brought in, and made fast to an opposite pillar; but we could not speak to, and could hardly see each other, as the yard was crowded with people anxious to get a peep at us.

† That is, one of the sailors or marines seconded from HMS *Melville*.

After standing here some time, a man came and took me away to another house, where, in the yard, was a quantity of cotton, and in one corner, looking out of a window, a Chinese gentleman and lady, before whom my guide led me, and prostrated himself, wishing me to do the same; but I contented myself with bowing, upon which the gentleman waved his hand, and I was led to the back-yard, where my guide brought me some rice and vegetables. I did not feel so grateful for my dinner as I perhaps ought, as I imagined this person had bought me for a slave.

When I had finished my repast, I was led back, and, being made fast to a tree, was left exposed to the mercy of the mob, without a guard. The people amused themselves with making signs; some, that my head would be cut off, others that I should not lose my head, but my eyes, tongue, nose, and all those little necessaries, and then be sent away—a most unenviable state to be reduced to. I was kept here some time, surrounded by a number of ugly old women, who seemed to take a delight in teasing me; but the most active of my tormentors was neither old nor ugly, being a tall and well-made person; her feet were not so misshapen as the generality of her countrywomen's; in fact, she was the handsomest woman I saw in China. At last a man came, loosed me from the tree, and led me off to a little distance; and while one man brought a stone block, another was sent away, as I imagined, for an axe, or some such instrument; before this block I was desired to kneel, but this I refused to do, determined not to give up my life in so quiet a manner as they seemed to propose. The messenger returned shortly, the block was taken away, and I was led out of the village.

Being now guarded by a dozen armed men, I was led along the banks of a canal until I came to a bridge, where I saw some of my companions in misfortune; I could only exchange a hurried word or two as they dragged me past, as I supposed, to the place of execution. I went on thus, with two more of the prisoners at some distance before me, stopping now and then, and imagining every stoppage to be the last, and that I should here be made an end of; but they still led me on, until we came to another village, or rather town,[†] and I was taken to what appeared to me to be the hall of justice. I was led to the back yard, and placed in a room, half filled with a heap of wood ashes. Here I found three more of the crew, in the same miserable condition as myself; but still, even here, we found some to feel for and relieve us a little, for, on making signs that my hands were bound too tight, one of the Chinese loosened the bonds, and afterwards went out: returning shortly with a lapful of cakes, he distributed them amongst us, and then procured us some water, of which we stood in great need, as we had had a long march under a broiling sun.

To judge from later descriptions, what Scott calls 'cakes' were most likely savoury steamed buns, much like today's *baozi* or *mantou*.

We had scarcely finished our cakes, when some of the soldiers came in, and took one of my fellow prisoners just outside the door; as I could observe almost all that passed, it was with feelings of the most unpleasant nature that I saw him made to kneel, and directly surrounded by the soldiers; one of whom came in, and took away a basket full of the ashes. I

† Possibly the walled town of Cixi, whose magistracy would certainly have struck Scott as a 'hall of justice'.

now supposed that we had come to the last gasp; I fancied my companion's head was off, and that the ashes were taken to serve in the place of saw-dust, to soak up his blood. I was not long kept in suspense, for the door opened, and some soldiers entered, who forced me to get up, and go out into the yard. I now took it for granted that my hour was really come; but, to my great relief, they had only brought me out to fetter me. They put irons on my hands and feet, those on my ankles being connected by a chain of five or six links, and an iron collar round my neck, with a stick fast to it, which was also made fast by a padlock to my handcuffs. I hardly knew whether to rejoice or not at this prolongation of my life, as I might be kept in this condition a short time, only to suffer a more lingering death in the end. When my irons were on, and rivetted, I was led into the outer yard, now crowded with people, and again tied up to a post. On looking around me, I saw my companion, who had been led out before me, fastened in a similar manner to the post opposite; and in a short time they brought the other two, and made them fast to the corresponding corner pillars. We remained a short time exposed to the insults of the lower orders, who amused themselves with pulling our hair, striking us with their pipes, spiting in our faces, and annoying us in all the petty ways they could think of. At last our guards came, and led us to a small room by the side of the gate, where we again had some rice.

When we had finished our rice, we were led through the town, down to the side of a canal, where boats were waiting for us. Into one of these they put me and a Lascar, the other two prisoners in another boat, each boat having a guard of several soldiers. We were towed, by one man, so quickly down the canal, that I had little time to notice the country, even had I been in a state of mind to pay much attention. I could see, however, that other canals branched from ours in every direction, and on the banks were an immense number of wheels and machines of various descriptions, for raising the water from the canals, and irrigating the rice-fields; some worked by men as at a tread-mill, and others by buffaloes, which walked round and round in a circle, as we occasionally see horses in our mills. By dusk, we arrived at a large town, where we had to change our boat; rather an awkward piece of business, as the guard would render us but little assistance, and, fettered as I was, I found it very difficult to crawl from one boat to the other. At last I managed it, and then lay down in the bottom of my new conveyance, the soldier taking the precaution of making my neck-rope fast, so that I could not escape.

About ten in the evening we arrived at another town,[†] but, being late, everything here was perfectly quiet. I was now landed, and led through the town to the mandarin's house; on the way there, I tripped and fell, breaking the rivet of my fetters, and cutting my knee at the same time. The soldier who was leading me by the rope round my neck, said nothing, but waited very quietly till I had picked myself up again, and we proceeded on, till we came to the head mandarin's house.

Here, to my great joy, I found the greater part of those who had come ashore in the junk with me; but still those who had got into the other boat, on leaving the wreck, and those who had run away, were missing; and we could hardly hope ever to see them again. I sat down on one of the steps, an officer brought me some cakes, and on seeing my knee, which had rather

---

† Yuyao, from where Anne too was taken by boat to Ningbo.

a deep cut, brought a small bottle, from which he sprinkled some kind of powder on the wound: this immediately stopped the bleeding, and in a day or two the part was healed.

This seemingly magical powder was possibly an effective astringent such as potash alum with a little 'dragon's blood' (a bright-red plant resin) added, a formula long used in China to stem minor wounds.

I sat here a short time, without being allowed to speak to the others; till suddenly we were made to stand up and place ourselves in two rows, and the mandarin and two of his officers made their appearance. They walked down the rows, stopping at each person, and by signs asked if we had had guns or opium on board our vessel. We only shook our heads in answer to their questions, and as we were not able to understand the other signs, they very soon retired.

When they were gone, the soldiers led us across one or two yards, into a jos-house [i.e. a Buddhist temple]. By the light from the torches, I could distinguish, in a place railed off from the rest of the building, some people lying apparently asleep. At first I imagined them to be Chinese; but to my amazement and great joy, I soon discovered this party to consist of Webb and Wombwell, and those who had left the wreck in the other junk, and of whose fate we had hitherto been in ignorance. In consequence of some misunderstanding, they had been most severely beaten by the Chinese, and from the effects of this beating two of the marines had died on their way from the coast to this town. Though dead when they arrived, the Chinese had, nevertheless, put irons on the bodies. The corporal of marines had been so ill treated, that he could not move without assistance;

and in fact they had all experienced worse treatment than our party.

None of the Royal Marines from the *Kite* were to leave an account of their experiences in China, so we can only guess as to why their party was so badly treated that some had died: dressed, as they must have been, in tight red coatees with facings and insignia, and with white trousers and black leather boots, even to an inexpert eye they must evidently have been military men, and obvious targets for the anger of the militiamen who had captured them. It is clear from Scott's description that the temple room they were now reunited in was a *tianwangdian* or Hall of the Heavenly Kings, which housed statues of Maitreya (the familiar 'laughing Buddha'), Wei Tuo the guardian of Buddhist teaching, and the deities who watch over the four cardinal directions.

In the morning, when I awoke, I found I was in a temple; outside the railing was a large hall; on each side, rows of seats were ranged, with a broad space in the centre; the sides of the building were quite plain, and so also was the roof. Inside the railing was a green silk canopy, under which were several images, handsomely dressed in different coloured silks. Standing against the walls were four more figures the size of life, one painted entirely black, another red, and the other two variegated; and all armed with some extraordinary instruments of warfare. These I suppose represented their gods, and were tolerably well done, but not to be compared to others I afterwards saw. The whole building was so destitute of any ornaments that had it not been for the images the idea of its being a jos-house would not have struck me.

The prisoners in their cages (from Scott's *Narrative*).

Breakfast was brought in early, consisting of sweet cakes and tea. When we had finished, two wooden cages were brought; the Chinese lifted one of our men into each, and carried them outside the gate, to be looked at by the common people; whilst the gentlemen, and better class, with their families, were admitted about two dozen at a time, to look at us who remained inside: sometimes we were visited by a party consisting entirely of women; they were a remarkably plain set, their pretensions to beauty, in their own eyes, appearing to lie in having the face painted red and white, and the feet distorted into a hoof-like shape. After keeping those in the cages outside for about two hours, they were brought in, and two fresh ones were taken out. Those who came in, told us that the bodies of our two poor fellows, who had been killed the day before, were lying outside on the grass, with the fetters still on. Fortunately it soon began to rain heavily, when the other two were brought in, and the crowd gradually dispersed.

About noon we had our dinner; one basin full of rice and vegetables, and cakes and tea, as before; our jailers would never give us plain water, but whenever we asked for anything to drink, brought us weak tea. For supper we had cakes and tea again, and, after this last meal, lay down on our straw for the night.

The next day was passed in a similar manner; towards evening there was a great mustering of cages in the hall; little did I think for what purpose they were intended. After the Chinese had ranged these horrible things in the open space in the centre, they made us all get into them, one into each. I forgot to say that before we were put into our cages, our jailers gave us each a loose jacket and a pair of trousers, besides as many cakes as we could carry. In these wooden contrivances we had neither room to stand, sit, nor lie, so that we were obliged to place ourselves in a dreadfully cramped position. Some few of the cages had a hole cut in the lid, large enough to allow the top of the head to pass out: into one of these I was fortunate enough to get; but those who were not so lucky, had the misery of sitting with their heads on one side, to add to their other discomforts. Afterwards I was put into one without a hole, and miserable was my position.

When we were all stowed in our separate cages, we were carried down to the side of the canal, and placed in boats, two cages in each boat, attended by a mandarin officer and several soldiers. My companion was a marine, one who had come ashore in the junk with Webb and Wombwell, and was still suffering from the effects of his beating, besides being almost dead with dysentery. We lay alongside the quay till nearly midnight, the soldiers and other people constantly running backwards and forwards on shore, with torches and gongs, shouting and making a great noise. About midnight we shoved off, and started down the canal; but as the junk was covered over, and it was very dark, I could see nothing of the country.

We soon appeared to be in a wider stream, as they made sail on the boat, and we went along at a rapid rate. In the morning I found that we had got out of the canal, and were in a river, going down with wind and tide. At any other time I should have enjoyed myself very much, but at present my future prospects were too far from agreeable to allow of anything approaching to enjoyment.

The banks of the river appeared to be well cultivated; here and there some military stations might be seen, distinguished from the other houses by their flag-staffs. Many junks were moored alongside the bank, some very large, one in particular, whose long streamers flew gaily out in the breeze.

We stopped at a town on the left bank, where the soldiers got some firewood, and immediately set to work to prepare breakfast; rice, and some compounds of I know not what, for themselves, and sweet cakes and tea for me and my companion; but he was too ill to eat, and was constantly craving for water, which was never denied him. On our arrival at this town, the people crowded into our boat, nearly capsizing her; and to my surprise our guards made no attempt to keep them out, but on the contrary rather encouraged them. They had not long to satisfy their curiosity, for as soon as the soldiers had procured all they wanted, the boat was shoved off, and they hoisted the sail again. We continued our way down the stream till we arrived at another large town on the left bank. Here we stopped again, and I could soon see we were to be disembarked. The people crowded to see us as usual, but one of the soldiers, throwing part of the sail over the tops of our cages, kept watch over us, and would allow no one to molest us.

John Lee Scott and his party had finally arrived in the city of Ningbo, the capital of the same prefecture within whose bounds Chusan lay and on whose coast the *Kite* had run aground. The 50-mile journey had taken them an entire week, and there were now worrying signs that the Chinese had gathered enough evidence to accuse them of having arrived with hostile intent:

> On the sail being removed, that we might be taken out of the boat, the first thing that met my eye was one of our guns, with the carriage belonging to it; soon after I saw another gun and its carriage. To enable the Chinese to get these guns, the tide must have fallen considerably after we left the wreck. The sight of these guns, as may be imagined, caused me anything but pleasurable sensations, as they proved beyond a doubt to our captors, that we had come to their coast with warlike intentions; and though they would perhaps be ashamed to kill a few shipwrecked merchant sailors, they might not hesitate to do so, if they could be certain that we had been concerned in the recent warfare, and these guns were strong evidence against us.
>
> On being taken out of the boat, a long bamboo was passed between the bars of my cage, and two men, placing the ends on their shoulders, lifted it off the ground; and in this manner I was carried through an immense crowd, the bearers sometimes stopping to rest, and placing my cage on the ground, upon which the people gathered round and began to torment me, as they had done in former cases. At length, after passing through a great many streets, some of them very gay, we arrived at an open space, at the end of

which were large folding gates; through these I passed, and after going up one or two passages, I found myself in a large hall. It was a large plain room, with a balustrade running down each side, behind which were several rough horses, saddled and bridled. At the end opposite the door was a large red silk canopy, under which was a small table, covered with a green cloth, and on it several metal plates and vases, dedicated to the *manes*[†] of the ancestors of the person to whom the house belonged. (I saw this kind of hall in every house I entered, and at the time imagined that it was dedicated to the Chinese penates; but I have since found, from Davis's *Chinese*,[‡] that it is called the 'Hall of Ancestors;' so throughout my story I have given it its right name.) Many of the prisoners in their cages had arrived before and the rest followed in due time. The Chinese ranged us in our cages in two lines, one on each side of the hall; and at the end of each line they placed one of the guns, with its muzzle towards us. When we were thus arranged, like beasts in a show, many well and richly-dressed people came to look at us; and none but the better sort seemed to be admitted, for, with the exception of the soldiers, there were no ragged people in the place. Our visitors were mostly dressed in fine light silks, beautifully worked with flowers and figures of different descriptions. All of them had fans, some of them prettily painted, and others plain. One or two of the men had enamelled watches, which they wore hanging to their girdles by a gold chain. We were treated pretty well by them, as they gave us fruit and cakes, and sent water to those who asked for it.

[†] In ancient Rome, the souls of deceased ancestors.
[‡] *The Chinese* was published in 1836. Its author, Sir John Francis Davis, had been Chief Superintendent of British Trade in China.

We did not remain long in this hall, for our bearers again made their appearance, and mine, shouldering the cage, marched off, and I was once more exposed to the mercies of the mob; the soldiers, our guard, never making the slightest attempt to keep the people off. Fortunately for me I had had my hair cut close only a few days before we were wrecked, so that there was little or nothing to lay hold of; for the people on one side would pull my hair to make me look their way, and those on the other side would instantly pull again, to make me look round at them; and I, being ironed, hands, feet, and neck, could not offer the least resistance, but was obliged to sit very patiently, or, in other words, to grin and bear it.

Heartily glad was I when again taken up and walked off with. After passing through many streets, I arrived at a mandarin's house, and was placed with the other prisoners in a small court. Some empty cages were standing about, larger than the one I was in, and with small yellow flags flying on their tops. In a short time some officers came in, and opening the lid of my cage, lifted me out, and led me out of this court into a larger one. To my great delight I here saw Twizell, and the three of the crew that had been missing, sitting in one corner, under a tree. I could not stop and speak to them, my guides hurrying me on. We scarcely recognized one another, so much were we altered.

I walked on for a short time, meditating on the past events, and wondering what my fate would be, when, raising my eyes from the ground, to my astonishment I perceived a man walking before me, heavily ironed, and whom I had never seen before. He was evidently an Englishman, and seemed almost in a worse condition than myself. When he heard me clanking after him, he turned round and spoke a few words, expressing his sorrow at seeing any one else in such a situation. I asked him who he was, and how he came there; but before he had time to answer, he was led down one passage, and I along another; so I could neither learn who he was, nor where or how he had been taken.

The mysterious 'Englishman' whom John had glimpsed was in fact Scottish, though he had spent little time at his ancestral home in Fife. His presence in Ningbo gaol was to make an enormous and very positive difference to Anne's life there.

Captain Philip Anstruther at the signing of the 1842 Treaty of
Nanjing (back row, second from left), and fighting off his captors
in *The Recreation* (1843). Given that Anstruther himself boasted
of being 'the ugliest man in the British army', depictions of him
do seem overly flattering!

5

'a small dirty room'

LIKE many of his fellow officers in the East India Company's army, Philip Anstruther had been born in India and educated at Westminster School before training at the Company's military seminary in Addiscombe, Surrey. Returning to India in 1824, he had been commissioned into the Madras Horse Artillery and made a captain fifteen years later while serving at the Royal Artillery Barracks at Woolwich (at just the same time, coincidentally, that the Chinese were destroying countless chests of British opium in faraway Canton). He seems to have been an endlessly inventive man, forever looking for ways to improve the effectiveness of his regiment's weaponry. Unhappy with the weight of his 18-pounder iron field guns (each of which demanded 38 bullocks to heave over India's unfavourable terrain!), he reamed out a smaller 12-pounder gun to take an 18-pound cannonball, sliced several feet off its muzzle, placed it upon a wrought-iron carriage—wood was then the norm—and presented it at Woolwich for testing. On the firing range, Anstruther's gun performed just as well as the heavier one he sought to replace, but there were concerns about its manoeuverability and the idea went no further. As to his prototype gun-carriage, it was feared that wrought iron was too vulnerable to being smashed apart by a single strike from a cannonball, and that idea too was shelved despite Anstruther's politely worded objections. A military man through and through, then, Captain

Anstruther must have struck the Chusanese as the very archetype of the foreigners who had arrived out of the blue to bombard them and invade their land. Thomas Lucas, a soldier who met him in South Africa a decade later, remembered Philip as

> an enormous man, a good six feet high and weighing some twenty stone, with a huge red beard, a deep rich voice and a sagacious massive face, brimming over with jollity. He had a habit when not otherwise employed of pacing restlessly backward and forward to the full extent of his long saloon which was connected by folding doors and having at either end a table with a bottle of sherry at one end and a bottle of port at the other... rolling forth one continuous stream of anecdote, fun and wisdom.[1]

In letters he wrote from Chusan which now survive in the British Library, Captain Thomas Pears of the Madras Engineers described Anstruther as 'the life of every party he joined'.[2] He was said to have aroused curiosity by always carrying a gold coin with him; one day, it turned out, a stranger had walked up to him in the officers' mess, given him a hearty slap on the back, and exclaimed: 'By God, Sir, you are uglier than I am, here's a gold *mohur* for you!'

On September 12th, 1840, Anstruther had celebrated his thirty-third birthday in his regiment's mess on Chusan. Three days later (so an army doctor who had accompanied the expedition to China, was to recall), an officer passing by the captain's tent

> was surprised to hear moaning and groaning within. Fearing some one was unwell, he immediately entered, and, to his surprise, perceived Anstruther on his bed, writhing as if from pain. On approaching he found

'Captain Anstruther, Madras Artillery, carried prisoner to Ningpo'
(by Edward Cree, © Henrietta Heawood).

Captain Anstruther in his cage in Ningbo (self-portrait).

him fast asleep; and on being awoke, he said that he
had been dreaming that the Chinese had surrounded
him while out surveying, that they were binding him
hand and foot, and that he was struggling to extricate
himself, when he was awakened.[3]

Anstruther's dream was told by way of a joke that night
at dinner, and nothing further was thought of it until
someone recalled it the following evening when it was
noticed that he was absent. His absence was down to the
simple fact that he had, indeed, been kidnapped.

That morning, Anstruther had set out with his elderly
Indian servant to survey the valleys north of Dinghai.
On a knoll overlooking the city he took bearings, then
dropped down into Qingling valley intending to follow the
lie of the land back to the artillery's encampment. As they
walked through a narrow, thickly wooded pass, however,
they became aware that they were being tailed. They
turned and made for open ground, but a Chinese soldier
rushed out from the crowd and struck out at the servant.
Anstruther drove him back with a spade, but with more
soldiers bearing down on them the two fled as best the very
overweight captain and the elderly Indian could manage.
With villagers now aware of the rumpus and gathering to
attack them, the Indian tried to run but was struck down
and beaten to death with rocks. ('I am thus particular in
naming the place and describing it,' Anstruther later wrote
in a letter, 'as I hope B____ will take a dozen or two of our
people, and go and burn the place where the rascals pinned
me.') Anstruther, expecting the same fate, fought as best he
could but was overpowered, tied up, gagged, and suffered
having his knees beaten until he could no longer stand to
flee. Placed in a palanquin, he was carried to the fishing
village of Cengang on Chusan's west coast and arrived in

Ningbo by boat the next day. There, he was unexpectedly reacquainted with a familiar face.

Willing to work for foreigners as a middleman and general factotum, Bu Dingbang was known to the British mercantile community in Canton simply as 'the compradore'. Having agreed to accompany the warfleet when it sailed for Chusan, on arriving on the island he had been sent inland to find provisions. He had proved far more successful as this task than any of the British troops, but in late July, just a few weeks after Dinghai's capture, Bu Dingbang had been kidnapped by a band of islanders, whisked off to the mainland, and imprisoned in Ningbo on a charge of treason. Had it not been for his language skills—though a native of Canton province, he spoke English very well—he might already have been executed. But while the British expedition boasted a small handful of Chinese speakers, Bu seems to have been—at least until a new interpreter arrived from Canton in January of 1841—the only Chinese Anglophone available to Ningbo's mandarins.

After being questioned (with Bu's help), Anstruther was taken to one of Ningbo's gaols. There, in addition to leg-irons (which he guessed weighed some eighteen pounds), an iron ring was fastened around his neck and he was placed in handcuffs that were in turn locked to a short stick fastened to his neck ring. He was then forced into a wooden cage just three feet high and less than two feet wide. For a heavily-built man of over six feet tall, this must have been torture. Anstruther, though, aware no doubt of his imposing and officerly appearance, was self-assured enough to rather shrug off his physical condition as little more than an inconvenience:

Next day I went again to the mandarin's, and in course of conversation he asked about our steamers. I offered to draw one for him, and did it. He became civil and friendly, and gave the compradore [Bu Dingbang] and myself a good dinner; after which I got some hot water, and washed off some of the blood and dirt of the struggle, found my head handsomely laid open to the bone, my legs and arms covered with bruises, but no wound of any consequence, and the very judicious diet of the prison soon cured all the bangs and bruises.

On the third day after his capture, Captain Anstruther was lifted once more from his cage and taken to another mandarin's residence, where he met seven of the *Kite*'s crew and learned of its sinking. He drew a map of Chusan harbour and the city of Dinghai, with all the British ships and tents added, and the mandarins seemed to warm to him. The next day he drew them a map of London—'Westminster Abbey, St. Paul's, Windsor Castle, and Buckingham Palace, all pleasantly situated in a park, with Grosvenor-place very well situated for viewing all four!'—and the next day a map of England, 'showing mail coaches and cattle somewhat larger than cities or towns'.

Lieutenant Charles Douglas, having survived the sinking of the *Kite* and having by now been brought to Ningbo, was that same day introduced to Anstruther. One can well imagine their surprise and delight as their conversation progressed: by sheer coincidence, Charles was nephew to Anstruther's friend Lord William Douglas, whose home was Grangemuir House in Fife, not two miles from Anstruther's ancestral seat at Balcaskie. Charles' explanation of how he was related to Lord Douglas could not have left Anstruther in any doubt that he was the only son—albeit illegitimate—of Lord Douglas' late brother, the

Lord Lieutenant of Dumfries and 6th Marquess of Queensberry. The Chinese, certain that Captain Anstruther was their most high-status prisoner, were never to discover that Lieutenant Douglas was, in fact, of aristocratic blood.

The remainder of the survivors arrived in Ningbo in dribs and drabs. On September 23rd, more than one week after the *Kite* had run aground, Anne and Chief Officer Richard Witts finally reached the city. The two lascars still with them were led away to be housed with John Lee Scott and the other soldiers and sailors. Witts, however, perceived by the Chinese to be a cut above the common prisoners, was put in a room with Douglas on the opposite side of the same courtyard. While these two were allowed out of their cages during the day and were free to wander in the yard, Scott and the others were kept in terrible conditions in one, long room which was subdivided into four cells by wooden gratings:

> In this miserable place we found eight more prisoners, some of whom had been for two months in the same sort of cages that we were in. We were placed in the small divisions, the coops being ranged round three sides of each compartment, the fourth side being the entrance. A chain was passed through each cage, and between our legs, over the chain of our irons; the two ends being padlocked together, we were thus all fastened one to another, and also to our cages.

Scott's guess was that the eight prisoners already in the room were lascars who had been captured while fetching water on Chusan, though they might equally well have been some of the *dhobies*—laundrymen who had followed the army from Madras—who had also gone missing.[4] Some of Scott's party had been badly beaten on the road to Ningbo—two of the marines had been stabbed with spears—and their corporal was so ill from dysentery that he would die during the night:

> He had entirely lost his senses, and was evidently dying fast; the maggots were crawling about him, and the smell that came from him was dreadful. Fettered as we were, we could afford him no assistance, and the Chinese merely looked at him, and then walked off, holding their noses.

When trying to picture the prisoners' accommodation in Ningbo, we should not imagine anything approaching the equivalent of the gaols in Victorian England, with their clanging doors, rows of cells, and uniformed warders—such places did not appear in China until the 1900s (and the first, in Shanghai, was built by the British). In the 1840s, Chinese gaols were still quite basic affairs, found for the most part within the official building used by the local magistrate; this, called the *yamen*, was the administrative centre of each county town, and besides rooms designated for the essential functions of local government it contained dozens more for every imaginable purpose—there were residential suites, kitchens, reception halls, shrines, pavilions, archives, a granary, an armoury, stables, gardens—and always a small gaol. The *yamen* was set out in a formulaic pattern, with civil functions on one side and military on the other; halls of audience to the south and sleeping quarters to the north. The gaol normally sat in the southwest corner and might contain several courtyards surrounded by buildings of varying impregnability, from open-fronted halls in which prisoners were free to wander,

Ningbo from the city walls, c.1870. The tall building is the Drum
Tower; the *taidao*'s residence, where Anne was imprisoned, is
indicated to its left (north) (© 2008 Royal Society for Asian Affairs).

through to dark rooms in which they were kept in chains;
some even had a designated *nülao*, or women's prison.

But while the common soldiers and sailors were soon
moved to such a public gaol attached to the county *yamen*,
Anne, Captain Anstruther, Lieutenant Douglas and Mr
Witts were all retained in the relative salubrity of the official
residence of the highest-ranking mandarin in Ningbo — the
taidao, or 'circuit intendant'.[5] Since the *taidao* was also
responsible for overseeing maritime affairs, his decision to
imprison the most valuable of the foreign captives in part
of his own residence is quite understandable.

Just as in England, where incarceration in and of itself
was not much used as a punishment for crimes until the
mid-nineteenth century (Millbank Penitentiary opened
in 1816, and its successor Pentonville only in 1842) gaols

in Qing-dynasty China generally housed people awaiting questioning, trial, or punishment. *Habeas corpus* was unknown, the accused could not expect to be investigated evenhandedly, and interrogation amounting to torture was an acceptable means of making a prisoner (or even a witness) confess. It was the norm for an accused person to be led to gaol with a chain around his neck, and in this regard Anne, John, and the rest were treated no worse than any other suspected criminal. If found guilty by the local magistrate, trivial offences were normally dealt with by a summary but often severe beating while being held face-down, more serious ones by beatings and long periods of forced labour. Other punishments were common, especially the use of the 'cangue' — a large, wooden block with holes for the neck and wrists, in effect a portable stocks which might have to be carried for days, weeks, or months at a time. Offences with greater legal repercussions were passed to a higher authority and were punished by beatings followed by forced labour or internal exile, or, as a final sanction, death by strangulation, beheading, or slow dismemberment. Punishment was done publicly, and Western visitors to China often commented upon men being led through the streets in a cangue, beatings in the street, and executions in the marketplace.

The writings of Anne Noble, Captain Anstruther, Lieutenant Douglas and John Lee Scott appear to cover all possible varieties of prison accommodation, and those they describe were certainly typical for the time: generally just one storey high, with wooden pillars supporting rafters on which was spread a layer of reed matting covered by black roof-tiles. The walls were sometimes wooden gratings, sometimes lath and plaster, sometimes brick. The room Scott was in 'was partitioned off from another, in which was a bed, with two or three chairs, and a small table.'

In this room lived an old officer, of some rank, I suppose, as all the soldiers, and our jailer, paid him great respect. Two young men came to see him every day; whom we used to see, standing up before him, with their hands behind their backs, like schoolboys, saying their lessons to him. It looked, as ours did, into a small court, in which, also, were some of the same kind of large pans for catching rain water, as those before mentioned.

The 'old officer, of some rank' was possibly the local *dianshi*, the district gaoler, while the man Scott calls 'our jailer' was possibly the warden who took care of day-to-day matters: he was 'an old man with a loud voice, a cross look, and a piece of thyme, or some other herb, always stuck on his upper lip' (presumably to mask the smell). Others though were more friendly:

In front of our room was one appropriated to the use of one of the keepers. An old man, hasty at times, when rather *fou*, but who always behaved civilly, and in general very kindly towards us. To the left of his dormitory was a passage that led to the cook-house; and to the right, another that led into a large yard, on each side of which was a spacious apartment, where their jos-ceremonies were performed. Outside our door was a passage, and a staircase that led to the upper story. The passage led down to another large yard, one side of which was walled up, and on the other was a large open room, containing chairs, tables, and sleeping couches, with cane bottoms; this seemed the guard-room, as soldiers were always there, playing with dice and dominoes; and their arms (match-locks, and bows and arrows) were scattered about. Beyond this room was another passage, which led to

the room where the sixteen Lascars were confined; a
smaller and far less comfortable place than ours.

This mention of the Indian lascars being held in worse
conditions than the Europeans reflects a particular aspect
of Chinese justice that struck Westerners as far from just:
people were not remotely equal before the law, and there
was no pretence that things should be otherwise. To the
Confucian mind, the very existence of legal rules and of
punishments for transgressing them was undesirable:
ideally, all people ought naturally to behave correctly
according to codes of propriety and ritual that were
ultimately expressions of cosmic harmony. On one level,
an act of punishment served to bring back the harmony
which had been displaced by an immoral action, and it did
not matter fundamentally whether the person punished
was the same person who had offended, or even whether
the punishment was remitted in some other way. All the
way though imperial Chinese history, there existed a formal
scale of fees which could be paid in lieu of punishment:
everything from a beating through to the death penalty
could be avoided if enough money was handed over, and
it was even acceptable for a guilty man to pay another to
suffer punishment in his stead.

In some ways, gaols in imperial China were more like
our own debtors' prisons of the eighteenth century than
the penal institutions of the nineteenth: places where
inmates were both incarcerated and free, and where status
and money could still be enjoyed. Just as in an English
debtors' prison—the Fleet and the Marshalsea are the most
infamous—inmates were expected to see to their own
needs, including food. Given their exceptional circumstances, though, food was provided for these foreign
captives. To begin with this consisted of two small basins
of rice and one of vegetables every morning and evening,

though fine, white rice served in wooden tubs was soon freely available, and 'a kind of stew, very much like old rags boiled, in one dish, and saltfish in another'. What precisely this unappetising stew consisted of is hard to say, but Scott seems to be describing either *fupi*—the dried skin of hot beancurd milk—or a local speciality called *meigancai*—leafy vegetables that had been dried, salted, and left to ferment. Once or twice, John Lee Scott and the other foreign prisoners even benefitted from their gaoler's offerings to his ancestors:

> The domestics having placed three tables in different parts of the yard, (one being exactly before our window), ranged round the edge of each nine basins, with chopsticks to all; they then filled the cups with hot rice, and covered the tables with plates of pork, fish, and vegetables, and by the side of every table placed a pile of thin paper. Before each of these tables the old gentleman knelt three times, bowing his head to the ground thrice each time; after this he filled a small cup with *samshu*, and setting fire to the heap of paper, sprinkled the *samshu* over the blaze. When he had prostrated himself before all the tables, and burnt the three heaps, he retired to his apartment, and the servants removed the whole apparatus. I suppose his devotions had made him charitable; for all the good things he had prepared for his deities, he distributed amongst us poor prisoners.

These were indulgences which Ningbo's Chinese prisoners did not expect to enjoy. Scott shared his yard by day with some of these, who slept in another part of the gaol:

> Outside was a covered passage, in which were several stoves; and here the greater part of the Chinese prisoners cooked their rice and other victuals. They

> had all chains on their legs, but were otherwise
> free; and they gave us to understand that they were
> imprisoned for smuggling opium, or for using it.
> Some were of the better class, being well dressed, and
> eating their meals with the mandarin of the place.

That 'better class' of prisoner would have bought this preferential treatment; by contrast, 'two of the commoner sort had lost their tails, and one was minus his nose, which gave anything but a prepossessing appearance to his countenance.' Though the ancient punishment of *yi*—the slicing off of the nose—was not officially sanctioned under the Qing dynasty, this man at least does seem to have suffered it. As for the two men who had 'lost their tails', all Chinese adult men (with very few exceptions) were required by law to shave their head leaving just a long, braided pigtail as a sign of obedience to their Manchu rulers. Not having a pigtail was a very serious offence, and having it cut off was a punishment in itself.

But if the foreign prisoners were in some respects treated better than the common Chinese, they also had to put up with those same prisoners' music-making:

> Soon after we had finished our breakfast..., some
> of the Chinese prisoners began to play on musical
> instruments, in different parts of the yard, and
> independent of each other. One of these instru-
> ments was something like a mandolin, and played in
> the same way; but it was a most monotonous affair,
> with trifling variety in the notes; and the song was as
> bad, a kind of sing-song noise, with very little preten-
> sions to the name of music. Another was a kind of
> small violin, played with a bow; the player could only
> produce a wretched noise. One man had a small fife;
> he was not a whit superior to his fellows, though they

seemed lost in rapture at their own performance, and remained strumming and blowing all day long, barely allowing themselves time for their meals.

While the lower-status prisoners—the lascars, and the rank-and-file Europeans—were living on top of one another, Anne was almost alone. She was put in a room next to Anstruther's, still chained and in her cage, and his reassuring presence proved to be an enormous comfort.

> At Ningpo I was sorry to find another prisoner, Captain Anstruther of the Madras Artillery, who has since proved to me a most kind and true friend; there was also the compradore [Bu Dingbang], whom I think you have some knowledge of. My most cruel sufferings were now at an end, and of course I felt more deeply my sad loss; yet I knew, that I still enjoyed many blessings. Captain A's prison was next door to mine, and I had the pleasure of seeing him often. The Mandarins gave me some Chinese clothes of the gayest colors; distressing as it was to my feelings, I was obliged to wear them, and I was put into, what the keeper styled, a clean prison with a woman to attend on me in my captivity.

Though she does not say so explicitly, Anne's distress must surely have stemmed from the jarring unsuitability of her new costume to her status as a widow: though the height of the Victorians' funerary culture was yet to come, Anne would have wanted to prepare a mourning dress of heavy, black crêpe, the antithesis of the brightly coloured robe—most likely of embroidered silk—that she was instead given. That her Chinese outfit would have seemed to her Western eye quite comical in its shape and decoration would only have made it more incongruous. Why she was not provided with suitable Chinese mourning attire is an intriguing question, for with the English-speaking compradore Bu Dingbang interpreting for her when she was brought before them, Anne's captors must have been aware that she had recently been widowed. In Confucian China, a wife was expected to mourn her late husband by wearing clothes of undyed hemp for three years (even if in practice this was shortened to just two). The most likely explanation is that her captors were perfectly well aware that the non-Chinese races each followed their own traditions rather than the correct rituals laid down by Confucianism's canonical texts, and that Anne had no need for a robe of white hemp; the epithet *yí* 夷, by which the Chinese referred to foreigners (it is often translated as 'barbarian'), implied an ethical rather than a technological backwardness.

The compradore, himself imprisoned close by her cell, showed Anne 'many and great acts of kindness'. As for the woman sent to attend on her, she was most likely a *guanmeipo*, a title that might be translated as something akin to 'official old mother go-between'. Responsible for looking after any women in the gaol, these *guanmeipo* had a reputation for being little more than brothel-keepers who abused their position by selling the women for sex. Anne, though she was far too important a prisoner for there to be any possibility of such overt abuse, was made to spend her waking (and sleeping) hours in conditions that were far from comfortable.

> After breakfasting with Lieut. Douglas at the Mandarin's, I went to my lonely cell, a small dirty room, two sides of which were a mere grating, in many places daylight appeared through the rafters, and it was scarcely fit to live in, its only furniture being my cage (in which I still slept at night, and into which I

was put whenever I went to any of the Mandarins;) a lamp, an old table, and a stool. For the first time after the wreck, I was enabled to undress myself and arrange my hair. I could not but rejoice when a large room was prepared for the three gentlemen to reside together in—Lieut. Douglas having been hitherto obliged to endure all the discomforts of the common prison—although it deprived me of the company of my friend.

After Anne had been in Ningbo for just five days, then, Philip Anstruther was taken from the room next to hers and installed where there was 'a fine place to walk in in front, the cages taken away, and good bedsteads placed for us, and all very much more comfortable.' Subsequently, he and Anne met only when they visited or dined with the city's various mandarins, 'which we did at first frequently, but after their curiosity was satisfied I seldom saw them'. The names of these officials are never expressly mentioned by Anne or any of the other prisoners; given that there were so many ranks of 'mandarin' (the word is not a Chinese one but a catch-all term derived from the Malay for 'counsellor'), Anne and the others would have been introduced to a succession of different people, including Deng Tingcai (Ningbo's prefectural magistrate), Li Shaofang (Ningbo's 'circuit intendant'), Urgungga (the provincial governor), Zhu Tingbiao (the provincial military commander), and doubtless many more. One man we can say for certain was among these mandarins was Shu Gongshou, who at that time held the post of county magistrate in Ningbo. Shu seems to have treated the prisoners well: an English naval officer who met him in Ningbo a few years later described him as 'much and deservedly respected', and noted that the British had interceded on his behalf with the emperor (who had wished him executed for the subsequent loss of

Ningbo to British forces) on account of his 'having shewn great kindness to Captain Anstruther, Mrs Noble, and other English prisoners'.[6] When Anne and the rest were taken to see the mandarins,

> they amused themselves by questioning us about Her Britannic Majesty and her government, the number of her navy and army, and the rank and income of the officers. Often I had to repeat my sad tale, particularly on the arrival of other officers; this I thought a great trial, especially when alone. Their inquiries about our respective families, were most minute: particularly what relatives we were to Queen Victoria, and whether I myself was not her sister, which, notwithstanding what was said to the contrary, I was declared to be. But it would be endless to repeat all the foolish questions they asked; however, they made notes of all our replies. Captain A. was generally employed drawing, and I am sure his great talent as well as the patience he exhibited often ensured us kindness. I dwell with gratification on those bright shades of my then dreary life. It was always with deep regret I saw the arrival of my little cage. I had the pleasure of receiving from the gentlemen's prison a note almost daily.

Astonishingly, given that these notes from Captain Anstruther and Lieutenant Douglas were written on small pieces of rice-paper, many have in fact survived, Anne having presumably taken them with her when she was finally released.[†] Anne spent some 150 days in Ningbo, and so the 39 handwritten notes must represent only a fraction of their original number. Nevertheless, they are

---

† They are now owned by a collector in the US.

the most precious of windows into life in the gaol, replete with incidents and concerns that are never mentioned by Anne or by John Lee Scott. Who acted as the deliverer of these notes—presumably in exchange for a few copper cash—we cannot say, but one at least was carried by 'a little boy', and the fact that Captain Anstruther was careful not to be caught in the act of writing another indicates that his gaoler was unaware that the three gentlemen were communicating with Anne and—though much less frequently—Henry Twizell and the others.

These secret notes reveal, for example, that the prisoners had plenty of health concerns; living in unsanitary conditions (though they did procure some soap by and by) and with little or no heating during a cold winter, minor ailments might easily have become life-threatening. At one point, Mr Witts suffered from an infected finger caused by cutting a nail too near the quick, but thankfully it healed. Captain Anstruther nursed a severe cold brought about (he believed) by smoking a damp pipe, while Lieutenant Douglas suffered with a sore throat (this seems to have been a constitutional weakness of his) and requested that the compradore Bu Dingbang prepare him a gargle of alum water and chilli powder. (Gargles were easily prepared and widely used to stop a sore throat progressing into a serious illness: *The Domestic Dictionary & Housekeeper's Manual* of 1842 recommended a mixture of vinegar, water, and cayenne, and alum was commonly added as an astringent.) Chilli powder was also part of the prisoners' diet as well as their medicine chest: the chicken curries brought by Bu Dingbang were often a bit too garlicky for the gentlemen's taste, but they did request that he add more cayenne. For breakfast they might be offered omelette and liver, and they enjoyed eating whatever fish they were given despite it always being very undercooked. Douglas asked whether

Bu Dingbang might now and then ring the changes by procuring some steak or mutton chops, or even meat puddings and pies. An unexpected part of their diet was milk chocolate, which was used to rally the health of sick prisoners as was the common practice at the time. Anne neither drank nor smoked and seems to have spent her hours reading or sewing, but Anstruther and his fellow officers managed to while away the days with cheroots, tobacco, beer, brandy, and Madeira wine!

Though we might have expected their gaolers to confiscate anything of value—Anne's wedding ring had, after all, been stolen—the three officers at least had plenty of money to spend. Trading their silver dollars (which were the most common medium of exchange in China) for strings of the native copper cash, they were able to send sufficient funds to Anne and the other prisoners to buy whatever they needed from the local market. Their gaolers, they were well aware, pocketed a commission on everything they asked them to buy, but this did put them in a happier mood and more disposed to treat their prisoners well.

But no amount of physical comfort could change the fact that Anne had suffered the sudden and traumatic loss of her husband and child. On October 19th, just one month after the sinking of the *Kite*, Lieutenant Douglas sent a note to try to console her. Anne's notes to Douglas are lost, but she had evidently sunk into a deep despair at her destitution, and he now tried as best he could to assure her that they would soon be free, and that her countrymen would rally round to comfort and provide for her. He would in time be proved right.

Although none of the other prisoners had suffered the same mental torment as Anne, their physical condition

A courtyard in the Neixiang county *yamen*, Nanyang. Neixiang's *yamen* is the best preserved in China, and gives us a good idea of the kind of room ('two sides of which were a mere grating') in which Anne was kept.

was certainly worse. 'Two days after the removal of the gentlemen from the common prison,' she wrote, 'all the remaining captives were taken to a far distant jail under the pretence of better accommodations, excepting two who were sick.'

> I had the melancholy satisfaction of seeing them passing my door, but was not allowed to speak to them; it made my heart bleed to observe their distressed looks and haggard countenances.

Among the men whom Anne watched being led away was the apprentice seaman John Lee Scott, who described what their new home was like:

> Two sides of the apartment, in which I was placed, were of wood, and the other two of white bricks; but

they were so thin, and so insecurely placed together, that it would have required little strength to shove them down. The floor was an inch thick in dirt, and the ceiling (which was a great height) covered with cobwebs. It was a place that we might have got out of with very little trouble; but when out, we should not have known which way to turn, if escape had been our object, and our dress and looks would have betrayed us instantly. The consequence of such an attempt might have been fatal; so that they had us as safely confined in this insecure building, as when we were in the cages, fettered and chained to one another.

The window was besieged all day by well dressed persons, who came to see 'the lions;' at first we only looked again, but getting bolder by degrees, we turned beggars, and from every fresh batch that came to the window, we requested something—either money, tobacco, or cakes, not being very particular: if they refused to give anything, we immediately slid the panels to, which most effectually prevented their seeing us, and the soldiers, our guard, very soon turned them out. Our grating was blockaded continually in this manner for more than a week, when the visitors ceased to come, and we were left in quietness.

Lice began to appear on the men.

Being in so crowded a state, and never allowed to go out of the room, on any pretence whatever, the air soon became very unwholesome; and animals, the natural consequence of such a state of things, began to show themselves, and, in spite of our utmost exertions, increased upon us; so that if the warm weather, which was very favourable to them, should continue, we stood a fair chance of being devoured alive. But our deplorable condition fortunately raised up another nation, which, though living upon the same body, made desperate war upon the other creatures, and by this means they kept each other under. The principal employment in the morning was to overhaul our clothes, and kill all we could catch—a most disgusting way of passing the time, but yet most necessary; the rest of the day was spent either in walking up and down the room, spinning yarns, or sleeping.

6

'great luxury'

ALTHOUGH the conditions for John Lee Scott and the other European rank-and-file were difficult—to say nothing of the Indians in their even smaller cell—matters did at least start to improve for Anne and the officers once an official line of communication was opened up between Ningbo and Dinghai.

On September 20th, a week after Captain Anstruther had gone missing, the commander of the British naval forces at Chusan had penned an angry letter to the Chinese: 'I discover that the authorities in Ningbo have been inciting the residents of Dinghai,' Sir Gordon Bremer complained (ignoring the fact that his own forces had thought nothing of firing upon those very same residents).

> They stop them from selling us food, and recently they kidnapped a compradore of ours. Also, on the sixteenth of this month, lawless brigands saw our officer Anstruther and his servant walking unarmed in the interior of the island, whereupon they seized them and took them to you, of this there is no doubt. You call yourself a great nation, yet it is truly unworthy of the name to behave like this. I demand the immediate return of Anstruther, his servant, and the compradore. If so much as one hair of their heads is harmed, then officers and men of this nation shall pour forth a righteous vengeance, wiping out the guilty and the innocent alike!

But Bremer's threat was born of frustration at his lack of options. He had met the previous day with Sir Humphrey Le Fleming Senhouse, the 59-year-old second-in-command of naval forces, and had vetoed Sir Humphrey's offer to sail HMS *Blenheim* to Ningbo and shell the city into rubble if the Chinese refused to release Anstruther: the Elliots were still hundreds of miles to the north, and Bremer had not been granted the authority to use military force in their absence.[1] His communiqué was now the first of many sent back and forth between Chusan and the mainland as the British tried to work out exactly what had become of Captain Anstruther. Passed to one of the small junks that still frequented Dinghai harbour, it was carried across Kintang Sound and handed to the mandarin commanding the forces at Zhenhai, one Lieutenant-Colonel Lin.[2] From Zhenhai it was rushed the twelve miles upriver to Ningbo, from where it swiftly found its way into the hands of Urgungga, the provincial governor. 'The compradore and the officer Anstruther are both here,' Urgungga confirmed, 'but it is not just Anstruther who has been captured by our Heavenly Dynasty. In all, we have captured more than twenty foreign men, both white and black, and one white foreign lady.' This mention of a white woman was the first official intimation the British had had that the crew of the *Kite*, which had failed to arrive back in Dinghai, might have fallen into Chinese hands. Up to that point, there had only been speculation as to their fate: the waters of the East China Sea were imperfectly charted, and there was every possibility that the *Kite* had gone down with all hands or was stranded upon another sandbank. Immediately aware that the Chinese held the trump cards, Senhouse responded to Urgungga in conciliatory tones. 'Possessing the sentiments of the compassionate in one's bosom is cherished by both Britain and China,' he wrote, and so I ask that you grant us a list of the names of those captured, and the circumstances of their capture, so that we might console their families. Please let us know the woman's name, and how she was captured. Was it upon a ship? or did her ship destroy itself upon your honourable nation's coast? It has never been the practice of civilised nations to detain an enemy's womenfolk. We are sure that the Great Qing dynasty sincerely wishes to act in accordance with the compassionate laws of all civilised nations, and so we earnestly request that you release this Englishwoman.

'I have received the honourable vice-commander's response, and its sentiments were most sincere,' Urgungga replied.

I perceive that you are the kind of man who knows how to act according to changing circumstances. I have learned that the woman's name is *Annanabu*, and that she is twenty-six years old. There are twenty-eight others.

The list of names that followed left no doubt that not just Anne but also Douglas and much of the *Kite's* crew were in Ningbo. The news was both welcome and worrisome: besides a restive population on Chusan and worsening sickness amongst their troops, the British now had to take account of the possible repercussions on the prisoners of their next move.

As soon as the British learned that Anstruther was being held in Ningbo, his good friend Captain Balfour of the Madras Artillery wrote to reassure him that his relatives would be told he was alive and well. The Chinese faithfully delivered the letter to Anstruther's cell. More letters, both personal and official, would follow: when the two British plenipotentiaries arrived back at Chusan on September 28th, Sir George Elliot lost no time in writing to the Chinese suggesting a face-to-face meeting. The Chinese agreed, and on October 2nd Captain Charles Elliot and his interpreter John Morrison landed at Zhenhai. Once the compradore Bu Dingbang (who had been led there in chains) had confirmed their credentials, Charles entered into talks with Yilibu—the emperor's special commissioner in Zhejiang—and the military commanders of Zhejiang and neighbouring Fujian—Zhu Tingbiao and Yu Buyun.

'The foreigners were polite and respectfully submissive,' Yilibu informed the emperor when the meeting was over. Elliot, he said, had insisted that Anstruther be freed, and that Chusan could not be handed back until then. The British, he said, were 'crafty and slippery in the extreme, adept at fabricating sophistries and glossing over things.' They kept on changing their minds, he complained, and it was hard to predict what their next move might be. During the talks at the mouth of the Peiho, Admiral Elliot had agreed to sail to Canton and carry on negotiations there, but now, Yilibu reported, the question of the prisoners' release had been raised as an excuse to linger in Zhejiang.

> Since Anstruther was captured, Bremer, Senhouse, and Admiral Elliot have asked for his release four times, while Captain Elliot did not shrink from landing at Zhenhai in person to plead on his behalf. This Anstruther must be a man most intimately connected to the foreign chiefs for them to have no choice but to beg for his release so earnestly.

Yilibu wrote to Admiral Elliot, expressing his bewilderment that the British could deny Chinese soldiers the right to seize members of an enemy force if they happened across them.

Anstruther was captured because he'd gone deep into the interior of the island to survey its geography, and Douglas and the rest because they'd gone ashore and disturbed our people. It's not as though there was no good reason for their being taken! Imagine now that some Chinese officers were to lead a party of soldiers to the places where your ships are at anchor: would you just stand by and allow it? or would you have them captured in just the same way?

Yilibu's argument was perfectly reasonable, but more to the point were a couple of simple facts: the Elliots were not going to achieve their war aims by tarrying at Chusan instead of sailing to Canton to carry on the negotiations, and there was nothing that could be done to free the hostages so long as the Chinese refused. Their personal safety and their living conditions in Ningbo depended on there being as much goodwill as possible.

As both sides tried to find a diplomatic solution to the stalemate, the lull in open hostilities allowed supplies to reach Ningbo gaol from well-wishers on Chusan. On October 8th, letters holding out hopes of release were delivered to Anstruther's cell, along with presents from his friends. Amongst these were some lady's riding shirts, which were duly passed on to Anne.[3] Anne herself was provided with a bedstead, which she found 'a great luxury, having hitherto lain on a dirty floor'. The compradore Bu Dingbang, back from Zhenhai, told Anne that in his opinion she would be free within three weeks. Douglas for his part was of the opinion that they would be free in ten days at the most,[4] and soon there were rumours in the gaol that mandarins had been overheard discussing a release within a day or two.[5]

But despite her hopes of imminent freedom Anne began to feel unwell, the pains becoming so violent that she was unable to lie down to sleep. So ill did she appear that her gaolers ignored their orders and removed her wrist-irons for a few hours. What precisely had caused her such pain is now impossible to confirm, but all the indications are that Anne seems to have believed herself to be pregnant.

After suffering that sleepless night she wrote to Lieutenant Douglas asking for advice; he wrote back suggesting she write to a Mrs Gutzlaff on Chusan as 'the most sensible person'.[6] He was referring to Mrs Mary Gutzlaff, the wife of Karl Gutzlaff, a Chinese-speaking missionary who had arrived on Chusan with the British fleet and who had rapidly made himself indispensable to the conduct of the island's military occupation. Though Karl was Pomeranian, Mary herself was English, and they had met in Malacca where she too had been working as an independent missionary and educator. She was an imposing woman, 'somewhat tall and well-built.'

> She had prominent features which were strong and assertive.... She had thin lips, supported by a square chin, both indicative of firmness and authority. She had flaxen hair and eyebrows somewhat heavy. Her features taken collectively indicated great determination and will power.[7]

With the upper ranks of the British community in China being relatively small, it would be no surprise if Lieutenant Douglas had met Mary in person and been struck by this air of businesslike competence. Anne now opened up a correspondence with Mrs Gutzlaff as Douglas suggested, and her letters soon found their way into the hands of an acquaintance of the Gutzlaffs who was also residing in Dinghai, a medical doctor named William Lockhart. In a letter home,[8] Dr Lockhart mentioned in passing that Anne was expecting to give birth sometime in April of 1841, and given that she had borne Ralph in the spring of 1840, a further conception that summer (two or three months before the *Kite* sank) would have been nothing out of the ordinary. For his part, Dr Lockhart had studied medicine at Liverpool University, had trained in Dublin and at Guy's Hospital, London, and was a member of the Royal College of Surgeons. He was certainly amongst the best-qualified of the Western physicians on Chusan, and Anne's letters must presumably have been passed to him for his expert opinion.

Yet even if he and Anne had been sat face-to-face in his consulting room, it is unlikely that Dr Lockhart would have been able to correctly diagnose the problem: severe pains during pregnancy can be caused by all manner of conditions, some quite harmless, some potentially fatal; in the mid-nineteenth century they were put down to 'the state of the bowels', 'errors in diet, or mental emotion', and the physician's first line of attack was 'to quiet the pain by a full dose of laudanum and ether'. Next might come purgatives to clear the intestines, a tonic made with bismuth oxide, the application of plasters impregnated with belladonna, or even a good bleeding with leeches.[9] But Dr Lockhart's surgery was 35 miles away, and with the waters of Kintang Sound between him and Anne he might as well have been on the moon.

So Anne was suffering all the discomforts of prison made worse by her physical condition, but her mental anguish seems to have been harder to bear. This was in a small way at least helped by being allowed to tend to the private soldiers and sailors who had been too ill to be moved out of the magistracy gaol: 'I was sometimes allowed to see and converse with the sick prisoners,' she wrote, 'and I almost felt a consolation in dwelling upon the dreadful past.'

> Frequently my heart was sadly torn, on account of different reports about my late dearly beloved husband and child. I was once told, that he was seen going to his cabin to rescue his child, and was afterwards seen dead with the baby on his bosom. Many were the sleepless nights that such accounts gave me, but I found subsequently—when meeting all the prisoners at the Mandarin's, and minutely examining into the fact—that this rumor was unfounded, for they had never seen the captain after the ship had heeled over.
>
> On the 14th, they sent another woman to wait on me, with a little cross boy about four years old, who cried the whole day long. This I felt a great trial, as I could not have a moment to myself, and, what distressed me most, my communion with God was interrupted. The other old woman brought also her girl, so that there were now four dirty creatures in my dirty hovel. This was scarcely endurable, but, after many entreaties and the lapse of a considerable time, both the children were removed. On Sunday the 18th, I heard the melancholy tidings of one of our sailors being removed by the hand of death. I had seen the poor boy several times, and, as I felt sure he could never recover, the few moments we were allowed to speak, were spent in dwelling upon solemn subjects. Though he was a mere skeleton and weak as a child, still he wore his irons to the last. A day or two before his death, he told me he knew that he would never be well again, but his mind was calm, and I fervently hope that the Saviour was present with him. As we parted for the last time, he said with much earnestness 'God bless you, Mistress,' these words I still remember, they

have been fulfilled, and God has remembered me. The two sick marines were much distressed at the death of the poor boy, and I was delighted to afford them some comfort, temporal as well as spiritual.

The 'ship's boy' whom Anne had comforted (his nominal rank hid the fact that he would have been in his twenties) appears to have been named Stanbury—a note sent by Douglas to Anne records his name, though the handwriting is unclear. He wasn't to be the last of the crew to succumb to dysentery, even though the Chinese did their best to treat them. The local doctors were familiar with the symptoms of dysentery and differentiated several different variations of the disease, each one treated with a specialized herbal preparation. Stanbury was given a bitter, brown medicine, but it ultimately did no more good than the primitive treatments—leeches and the like—which the British were using on Chusan.

In late October, Anne's situation unexpectedly changed very much for the better. Captain Elliot's face-to-face meeting with Yilibu at Zhenhai had engendered a great deal of optimism on the part of the Chinese, who were eager to make the British see that friendly diplomacy might lead to a speedy resolution. Yilibu, despite his distrust of the Elliots' unpredictable nature, was willing to hope that if and when they sailed south to Canton to discuss terms they would take the entire British force with them; already, some of the ships at Chusan had weighed anchor and left.[10] An end to the impasse seemed to him to be close, so long as the British took the sensible option and evacuated Chusan.

So when, one evening in late October, Anne and most of the other Europeans—two marines were still sick with dysentery—were summoned to see the *taidao* they were carried not in cages but in comfortable sedan chairs. Passing through a succession of gateways and courtyards, they were led around an ornamental rock garden and finally into the presence of the city's highest mandarins. The audience took place in what John Lee Scott recalled was 'rather a large chamber, open in front, as it was the hot season; several couches, and glazed arm-chairs, were arranged about the room; four large paper lanterns were suspended from the ceiling, and as the evening drew in, they, and many more placed in other parts of the room, were lighted.' There was a great deal of bowing and tea-drinking, and then the Chinese got down to business.

Letters had arrived from Chusan, and supplies that Lieutenant Douglas had asked for: a number of chests contained clothing and alcoholic drinks, along with three hundred silver dollars and plentiful clothes for the officers and for Mrs Noble.[11] Amongst the latter were shoes from Anne's friend Captain Baily and baby clothes for Ralph, sent by a Mrs Proudfoot.[†] 'The sight of clothes, intended for my dear lost one,' Anne was later to recall, 'was overwhelming. May the Almighty reward the kind donor and, by his gracious and merciful providence, ever protect her from requiring such a comfort, as she bestowed upon me.' For the common soldiers and sailors, however, there was nothing, even though Lieutenant Douglas had asked his friends on Chusan to send clothes for them as the weather was set to grow colder. The Chinese, observing that most of the men ranged before them had nothing substantial to wear, sent for baskets of clothing and gave

† There is no more detail on Mrs Proudfoot, but she might have been the wife of one of several Captain Proudfoots who can be found in the newspapers' *Shipping Intelligence* trading around the Indian Ocean and South China Sea at the same time as the *Kite*.

each of them a large, loose coat and a pair of warm, cotton-padded dungaree leggings. 'They were very warm,' wrote John Lee Scott,

> and well calculated to keep out the cold, but very clumsy and heavy; still they were not to be refused, and indeed had it not been for this kindness of the mandarins, we should have been exposed, almost naked, to the approaching inclement season.

To everybody's enormous relief, the shackles they had been wearing since being captured were now taken off—with the notable exception of the two surviving marines, whom the Chinese clearly resented. Bu Dingbang, who had been brought from the gaol to interpret for the prisoners, explained that the Indians too might have theirs removed 'if they made no *bobberee*'.† (In fact, the Indians were obliged to wear their irons for almost the entirety of their time in Ningbo. They were clearly looked down upon by the Chinese as the physical and cultural inferiors of the Europeans—they had dark skin like the demons of Chinese folklore, were slight of frame, ate their food with their hands, and spilled precious rice on the floor.) The Europeans were also told that they could expect to be free within five or six days. Anne's reaction to the news was mixed:

> Gladness then pervaded every breast, but, as usual, mine was mixed with bitter grief, to think how short a time since a happy wife and a joyful mother, and that I must now return desolate and alone. However, I could but be thankful to be freed from my fetters, having worn them, as I imagine aright, for thirty-two

† A tumult or noisy commotion (an Anglo-Indian word).

days; and on our way home, if our wretched prisons
deserve such a name, our hearts were much lighter
and we began to put confidence in the glad tidings.

In a nearby room, plenty of good food was provided
for those prisoners who had neither money nor provisions—hard-boiled eggs, chicken, pork, steamed buns, and
meat dumplings—and Scott was given a handful of copper
cash by a well-dressed man in exchange for writing a few
lines in English upon a piece of paper. When he returned
to his cell, though, his delight in receiving warm winter
clothes was tempered by what he discovered living in them.

> With the new clothes came also some of those horrid
> creatures by which we had been tormented; these
> coming fresh from the tailors' hands, made us observe
> our guards a little more closely, and we could plainly
> discern that they were swarming with vermin. We
> were glad to find that what we had at first set down to
> our own dirt and unwholesomeness, was more attrib-
> utable to the dirt and laziness of our jailers and other
> people. Even the walls had their inhabitants, for they
> fell down out of the rafters upon us.

In anticipation of being released, Anstruther, Douglas, and
Witts set about working their way through their newly
acquired supply of alcohol and tobacco. But the 'five or six
days' came and went, and by the middle of November they
had smoked their last cheroot, Anstruther had caught a
cold, and there only remained three bottles of brandy to
console themselves with.[12] Despite this disappointment,
by exchanging their silver dollars for the copper cash the
officers were able to obtain little extras such as bread and
soap, some of which, along with 3,000 copper cash to see to
her own needs, they passed to Anne. To each of the white

prisoners they distributed 400 cash, and to each of the Indians 300, so that even they were able to buy a modicum of comfort.

Anne sent out for purchases in the bazaar; she bought a needle and thread, and applied her skills as a dressmaker to making clothes for herself, mending the men's tattered clothing, and lining their jackets for the approaching winter.[13] One item she was unable to make from what material the mandarins had given her, however, was a mourning dress fit for a woman who had lost her husband and son (it will be recalled that she had been distressed at having to wear 'Chinese clothes of the gayest colors'). On this point Captain Anstruther was able to be of help, and he arranged for $11 to be paid to a man he called 'Foo Ling' to provide suitable black silk and crêpe. 'Our life was now pleasant enough,' he wrote:

> I had writing materials and plenty of leisure, so I set to work to ornament the walls of my prison with drawings of my 18-pound gun and other diagrams connected with the noble science of gunnery. I flatter myself I have set forth the true theory of recoil in a new and striking light, and will astonish the artillery world with a treatise on carronades, which will make W___ bite the finger of vexation with the tooth of envy. I had to draw portraits of all the mandarins, pictures of Admiral Elliot, Capt. Elliot, the Queen, and a thousand other things, and so the weary, weary time passed slowly away.

Now that Anne and the officers had sufficient money they were able to eat well, with the compradore Bu Dingbang proving to have rather a talent for cooking. Captain Anstruther was even able to request that Bu use a little less garlic and a little more chilli in their curries, while Douglas was able to turn his nose up at a dish of liver which arrived one day at breakfast-time. Anstruther, a very capable artist, was also paid in food for his portraits of Ningbo's mandarins:

> There is an amusing anecdote told of him when in confinement, which is said to have come in a private letter from himself. One day a mandarin sent him a very savoury stew, garnished with sharks' fins and birds' nests, in compensation for a likeness which he had taken of the nodding gentleman. Anstruther having tasted the delicious contents, gave an inquisitive look at the attendant, and pointing to the stew, said 'Quack, quack, quack?' The servant shook his head, and replied, 'Bow, wow, wow.'[14]

But although he, Anne, Douglas and Witts continued (despite heavy colds and sore throats) to be 'well, hearty, and as happy as prisoners can be', some of the others were in Anstruther's opinion still being treated shamefully. In early November, the two marines suffering from dysentery had finally been removed from the county magistracy gaol and taken to the same gaol as the other rank-and-file sailors. One of them, 'owing to a good constitution, and the kindness and attentions of Mrs Noble, who did all that possibly lay in her power to alleviate their sufferings, had rallied and was now looking well', thought John Lee Scott, but the other was so ill that Anne could only watch from her cell as he collapsed while being led away. The cell for these two sick men had been so small that they had been unable to turn around without disturbing the other, and they had not once been allowed out to get a little fresh air and exercise. When they arrived in their new prison, Scott was shocked by the appearance of the one marine who had grown even sicker. He presented a most horrid spectacle, a moving skeleton, with the skin stretched tightly over his bones; his eyes were sunk deep in his head, and his voice was awfully hollow; he was the most melancholy sight I ever saw. When on board the ship he was a stout, well-made man, and now how dreadfully changed! he had come up merely to die with his old companions.

News of his death soon after 'affected us all deeply', wrote Anne,

and especially his master [i.e. Lieutenant Douglas]. Death has made sad havoc amongst us, and the Almighty alone knows the reason why he afflicted us, and I fervently hope that these many solemn warnings may be sanctified to us.

As the days and weeks dragged on, John Lee Scott for one 'gave up all hopes of a speedy release, expecting nothing less than an imprisonment of a year or two'. He and his fellow prisoners amused themselves by watching their guards fighting in the courtyard of the gaol. It was, in his opinion, 'a most unpleasant kind of combat',

for they seized hold of each other's [pig]tails with one hand, and dragging the head down almost to the ground, clawed and scratched with the other hand, till the one with the weakest tail rolled over and gave in; we always tried to get out and see fair play, but the soldiers mustered too strong at these times. Sometimes, again, a drunken soldier would make his appearance, and coming to the window afford us a little amusement, for, getting hold of his tail, we made it fast to the grating, and then left him to get loose as he could; generally one of his comrades, attracted by his bellowing, came and released him.

At other times they took advantage of the fact that their gaolers had grown 'rather free and easy' with them. One day,

> one of our party slipped out into the passage, whilst the servants were removing the rice and dishes, and brought in the piece of bamboo and stick, which the watch used at night; in the evening we saw the soldiers searching for it, but we kept quiet till dark, and then we began to keep watch ourselves; but the noise soon brought our jailer in, who took the bamboo away, threatening to put us in irons. This threat made but little impression, for, a short time after, another of the party walked off with a teapot belonging to one of the soldiers; this we kept for several days, till the owner found out where it was; but we would not give it up unless he paid for it, and as our jailer and his own comrades only laughed at him, we obliged him to redeem his teapot with a hundred or more pice, much to his dissatisfaction. ... One evening, whilst at our supper, one of the soldiers came to the window, and amused himself by imitating our awkward attempts to eat with the chopsticks. This impertinence so incensed one of our men, that he jumped up, and filling a basin with water, dashed it through the bars into the soldier's face, taking him quite by surprise; the water streamed down his breast, inside his numerous jackets, and must have made him most uncomfortable. But his only revenge was swearing and shaking his fist at us as he ran away. Finding that no harm arose from this first attempt, we determined never to be annoyed again, regretting that we had allowed ourselves to be overlooked so long; therefore all parties that would not pay for peeping, we drove away by throwing water at them; and having a bucketful in the room, the water was always at hand.

Our proceedings amused the old jailer exceedingly, and he very often brought people to see us, and then getting behind them, made signs for us to throw the water in their faces; taking care, however, always to get out of reach of the shower, and to condole with the visitors, who generally received a good ducking.

'All this,' Scott admitted, 'was not very edifying employment, but it served to pass the time, which, having no books or employment, hung very heavily on our hands.'

The weather grew colder, with occasional falls of snow, but at least the temperature made the insects that infested the prisoners' clothes torpid and their bites more bearable. The few pieces of charcoal which their gaoler handed out did not last long, and so the floorboards and even the bars of the men's cell door were broken up and burned.

Our room was too crowded for us to feel the cold much, but still it was rather chilly; so, to keep ourselves warm, we ran round and round our apartment, played at leapfrog, and such other games, which kept the blood from freezing in our veins; besides, we bought pipes and tobacco, and constantly smoked, which warmed us a little, and probably prevented sickness getting in amongst us; this was a great advantage, for if any fever had broken out, we might all have been carried off, from the extreme unwholesomeness of our apartment.

With just two meals each day—usually plain rice, enlivened now and again with 'turnips, and very small fish'—the men took to hiding some of their morning rice ration to enjoy at noon. As Christmas approached, they bought a little meat with the cash passed to them by Lieutenant Douglas and coaxed their gaoler into giving them some *samshu*.

We made a better Christmas of it than I had expected, and after our dinner we called our jailer in, and drank his health, to his great delight; in fact, he was so much pleased, that he ran out of our room, and immediately returned, bringing with him a haunch of goat, which he said 'he gave to us'; and was going to hang it up in our room, but we deemed it expedient to place it in the outer air, so he hung it up outside, and we had it for dinner the next day. From this time we were allowed to have as much *samshu* as we liked; and with the exception of one Lascar getting drunk, no one ever forgot himself. The Lascar, when he came to his senses in the morning, we tried by court-martial, and sentenced him to receive three dozen, which were administered with a cat made for the purpose, of threads twisted and plaited together.

The one surviving marine was now the only European still in shackles. Unhappy at how the mandarins had reneged on their promise to Lieutenant Douglas to take them off, the sailors now took it upon themselves to pick the padlock and hide them under the floorboards 'as a legacy to the rats'.

7

'an inestimable treasure'

OUT of the blue, one day in December a man who
struck Anstruther as 'an ugly vagabond' came to the
grated door of his room and slipped him a note.† It had
been sent by Colonel Patrick Montgomerie, commander of
the Madras Artillery Regiment on Chusan, who had been
organising the supplies which had so far reached Ningbo.
But while letters and supplies addressed to Ningbo had
been duly delivered (though not without a degree of
pilfering) letters from the prisoners to their friends on
Chusan had not. Now, though, with this local man able to
move unsuspected between the Chinese and British camps,
the prisoners could write without fear of their letters being
intercepted: 'Our joy was inexpressible,' Anne recalled.
Anstruther dubbed their go-between 'Blondel', after the
faithful squire in a popular comic opera of the day called
Richard Coeur-de-Lion.[1] 'We hope for an early release now,'
Anstruther wrote in the first of the letters which Blondel
was to carry back to Dinghai,

> but in case we should not get it, pray send my Bible,
> and one or two more for the sailors and Mrs. N.; and
> for me send Gibbon's *Decline and Fall*, in one volume,

† McPherson says it was Anstruther who first employed 'Blondel',
 sending Montgomerie a note in November; Anstruther and Scott
 disagree, saying that he turned up in Dinghai offering to act as
 messenger and that the British had bribed him.

and any other works with much in small bulk, and *no pictures*. Please send me a knife *concealed*, and some shirts; no more wine; but any other little refreshments you like. A thousand thanks to you, Barrow, Balfour, Grant, and all Gunners and Sappers, for what you have sent me. Douglas wishes Mr Porter, the purser of the *Blonde*, to send him a blanket, frock and trousers, and an anker[†] of rum. I am very busy writing *A Treatise on Carronades*; so pray send me another steel pen (mathematical) and some paper.[2]

Blondel made the forty-mile voyage to Dinghai, passed the letter to Colonel Montgomerie, and Anstruther's Bible and knife duly arrived just a few days later along with a letter for Anne from Mrs Gutzlaff which, she wrote, 'afforded me very great consolation'.

It struck Captain William Caine, who soon after the invasion of July had been appointed Chief Magistrate of Dinghai, that an insider like Blondel would be able to provide useful intelligence on the prisoners' situation. In early January, Captain Caine questioned Blondel and learned that Anstruther, Douglas and Witts were being held just a short distance from Anne, with some seventeen or so guards watching over them. One of Ningbo's rivers ran close by, with boats manned by more guards. But most of the guards were either friends of Blondel or else were obliged to him for assistance he had given them. One hundred and fifty silver dollars would be enough to bribe them all, he said, and if a note could be sent to those four prisoners explaining that a boat was waiting for them then it would be possible for them to escape. As for the others, they were being held at a distance in a prison that was more exposed to public view, and it would be best to

† A cask holding slightly less than a firkin, or around 39 litres.

No doubt a familiar scene to Anne and the other prisoners: one of the many canals that once flowed through Ningbo (c.1870) (© 2008 Royal Society for Asian Affairs).

rescue Anne and the officers before attempting this more difficult exploit. Blondel left any reward for his services to the generosity of the British, asking only that a relative of his, who owned a timber yard in Dinghai, be allowed to remove his property from the city.[3]

The escape plan was put to the three gentlemen in a letter which Blondel carried to Ningbo, but Captain Anstruther vetoed it: he himself could escape without help, he wrote via Blondel to tell his friends on Chusan (with a comical disregard for how conspicuous a six-foot foreign soldier with a big, red beard would be!), but Douglas and Witts would suffer as a result; all three of them could try to escape, but then the retaliation would fall solely upon Anne, who Anstruther understood to be heavily pregnant. She was in no fit state to escape, and Douglas wouldn't go without taking the survivors from the *Kite*. The European prisoners, now ten in all, were a mile away, and the Indians, numbering between fourteen and sixteen he thought, were near them. 'We would perhaps agree to leave the niggers,' he wrote, his choice of words jarringly racist to our ears but quite normal for his day, 'but even the other three detachments could hardly all succeed, and we must all or none escape, so I fear it is out of the question.'[4]

Anstruther's appraisal of the dangers of trying to escape were shared by Anne. On January 9th, she received via Blondel more letters from Mrs Gutzlaff, 'from one of which I learnt our then contemplated rescue, which at that time gave me great uneasiness, as I trembled at the idea of any of my dear countrymen running the risk of such sufferings as I myself had undergone.' She also received, at last, a copy of the Bible:

> an inestimable treasure for which I had so long and earnestly prayed, but, to avoid discovery, I had to read it during the night, so that it was in truth a secret treasure and henceforth my constant companion. It is wonderful how often we heard of our speedy release and were as often disappointed, still for the time being our spirits were kept up by these good news.

Rumours of a possible release, and disappointment when they turned out to be false, were to arrive frequently during the first weeks of 1841. In late November, the emperor's representative Qi Shan had arrived in Canton, having travelled overland from Beijing. Before the peace talks had even started, Admiral George Elliot, who for weeks had been suffering from a heart complaint, had decided to sail for Macau to recuperate, leaving his cousin Captain Charles Elliot as Britain's sole negotiator.

Once the talks began, Captain Elliot and Qi Shan soon agreed on compensation to cover the value of the destroyed opium and the costs of the war. The first intimations that terms might be agreed in Canton reached the prisoners a few weeks later. One day in mid-January, John Lee Scott and William Wombwell were taken before a mandarin and asked to explain the contents of some letters that had arrived via Chusan. When they were returned to their cell that evening, they were able to tell their fellow prisoners that there was every chance of peace, and of a swift release. When the letters were passed to the three officers and to Anne, they too learned that there were high hopes of an end to their imprisonment.

But with a great deal of mutual mistrust, the talks in Canton were never going to be straightforward. On Captain Elliot's other demands—the permanent cession of the island of Chusan to Britain, for one, and the opening up of China's ports to British merchants—Qi Shan stood firm: handing over a portion of sovereign territory to the British, and allowing them to trade as they pleased up and down the coast when they had already proven themselves to be so avaricious and violent were not points on which China was willing to bend. Soon after the commencement of the new Chinese year of the ox on January 23rd, Scott and Wombwell were again sent for by the mandarins. They found that more letters had arrived from Chusan with news of hope for a speedy resolution to the talks,

> but in one of the letters was a Latin quotation, which led me to suppose that peace was not quite so close at hand as the English part of the letter gave us to understand. ... Time passed, and we two paid several more visits to the mandarins, when we always heard the same reports of liberty.

Given the length of time it took for news to reach Ningbo gaol from the mouth of the Pearl River, the prisoners were fully aware that events on the ground could move faster than a handwritten letter, and they remained sanguine about the possibility of imminent freedom. Their attitude was justified: while in Ningbo the Chinese New Year was being celebrated with rockets and firecrackers, 800 miles away there had been more fighting.

On January 5th, tiring of Qi Shan's refusal to grant him what he wanted, Captain Elliot had ordered the Royal Navy to destroy the forts commanding the river passage to Canton. Believing the heavily entrenched works to be impassable, the Chinese had been stunned when they were shelled into rubble within ninety minutes. The next day, with warships moving against a second line of defences, the shocked Chinese had called for a ceasefire. Deploring the slaughter, Elliot had agreed to start talking again. From that point it had taken less than a fortnight for a settlement to be agreed. Qi Shan had ceded Hong Kong to the British as a trading station; a $6,000,000 indemnity would be paid for the opium; official intercourse between the two nations would henceforth be carried on as between equals; and the Canton trade would restart after Chinese New Year on a secure footing. And as part of the agreement, the prisoners languishing in Ningbo were, of course, to be released. In return for all this, Chusan was to be evacuated, and the steam sloop *Columbine* was duly sent north to inform the garrison of the news. In the meantime, however, life went on as normal for Anne.

> On Tuesday the 2d of February, I heard that the gentlemen had been summoned by the Mandarins to receive clothes and letters, and with an anxious heart I watched the whole afternoon, expecting every moment a visit from them. However, I was obliged

to continue in suspense till the next day, when I was called to appear before the Mandarins to obtain another most affectionate letter from you, my dear friend, with an abundant store of clothes and every comfort I could desire. Grateful and thankful as I felt for them, my spirits became deeply affected, inferring as I did, that so many things would not have been sent, if my captivity was not to be prolonged; yet the linguist [Bu Dingbang] cheered me by the assurance, that I should be free within three weeks or a month. At this time they treated me with great kindness and I went to see the Mandarin's lady, who gave me some fruit and artificial flowers, the first mark of kindness I had received from a lady. They allowed me to remain until the evening, and I was once more gladdened in meeting my countrymen, and, after staying some time, we all went to my prison to write answers to our letters.

Only on February 8th did Anne get word directly from the Chinese that she was to be released.

I had the pleasure of a visit from some Chinese naval officers, who told me, that we were to leave Ningpo within a fortnight. We thought there was truth in the news, but we were not certain until the 14th, when I received the glad tidings from [Mrs Gutzlaff]. It would be impossible to describe, what our feelings were on that occasion. I had thought that the gentlemen had known it the day before, so that our meeting at the first moment, was not so joyful as it otherwise would have been, but they had no sooner read my letter, than our mutual congratulations were warm and most sincere, and I again had the happiness of welcoming them to my poor prison, where we wrote answers to our friends. Nothing was now spoken of,

but the surety of our now speedy relief; as for myself I
could scarcely believe it.

One by one the guards began to pack up their few worldly
possessions and leave, trying to make it known to the
prisoners that this time they really were on the point of
being released. Still, when freedom finally arrived, its
suddenness came as a surprise. And of all people, it was
the emperor's special commissioner Yilibu whom they had
to thank.

By February of 1841, the emperor had run out of patience
with the elderly Yilibu for his failure to deal with the British.
For months, his memorials to the throne had promised
that great armies were preparing to retake Chusan, but
despite the funds that had been lavished on him the British
were still in control of the island and calling the shots in
Canton. Yilibu was replaced as special commissioner by a
mandarin named Yu Qian, an erudite Mongolian high in
the emperor's personal favour, who was said to be proud
and overbearing, feared for his strict application of the
law, and eager to put the British in their place: they were
to him 'mere bulrushes' to be scythed down, and soon they
would be 'like moths to his flame, fish caught in his nets'.
Yu Qian set out for Zhejiang, boasting of how he was going
to execute the prisoners and display their severed heads in
cages.

Yilibu was more realistic about what the result of such
hotheaded violence would be: most likely, the British would
use the murder of the hostages as a pretext to launch an
even more devastating assault on the Chinese and increase
their demands. Negotiation and concessions had brought
the two sides to the brink of peace, and so, with Yu Qian
now bound for Ningbo and threatening to put Anne and
all the others to death, Yilibu ordered them to be released,

taken with all haste to Zhenhai, and put in boats before Yu Qian could get his hands on them.

When, before dawn on February 21st, the little boy who had been attending on the European sailors pulled back the shutters and tried to wake them up, all he received for his efforts was a volley of shoes. Then their gaoler arrived and made signs to the effect that they were leaving, and that he was to go with them. At first, the prisoners assumed that Lieutenant Douglas had persuaded the Chinese to move them to a better prison, but even this was good news and they began to pack their belongings. Outside, though, it became clear from the general state of confusion and the sheer size of the crowds that something more important than a change of accommodation was afoot. Each one now in his own sedan chair, they were carried through the streets and out of the city. Soon they had been ferried across the Yuyao River and from the far bank were able to look back at the place which for five months had been their home. What struck John Lee Scott especially was the ruinous state of the walls, which in parts were almost falling down.

It was a cold day, with a stiff breeze, and rather than freeze in their open sedans the men kept warm by walking briskly beside them. At dusk they reached the walled garrison town of Zhenhai that guarded the river approach to Ningbo, and there, in a Buddhist temple, they found Anne, Mr Witts, Captain Anstruther, and Lieutenant Douglas. The Indian sailors at last had their shackles removed—they had been wearing them ever since their capture and must have been suffering terribly from sores—and a newly arrived Chinese interpreter addressed them in their native Bengali for the first time.

In the middle of the night, with the tide rising, the prisoners were led down to the water between two long files of soldiers. The army which since July had tried—and failed—to dislodge the British from Chusan consisted of 'most unmilitary looking warriors; their only uniform was a loose jacket, with some Chinese characters inscribed on the back and front; the rest of their dress seemed left to their own taste, and a motley group they were.' Some carried long and unwieldy spears, others bows and arrows, while others held a sword in each hand. The paucity of their weapons only went to underline how important the capture of three white officers and a white woman had been in turning the tide of the war thus far in China's favour.

It was at around three in the morning that the tide was high enough for the junks to sail, Anne and Mr Witts together in one, the twenty-two Indians in another, and Anstruther, Douglas, Scott and the other Europeans in a third. At around ten the next morning, when the junks entered the harbour at Dinghai, the sailors on board the transports and the men-of-war began to cheer and the

The Salt Gate, through which the prisoners finally left the walled city of Ningbo (c.1870) (© 2008 Royal Society for Asian Affairs).

bands struck up *Rule Britannia*. 'What my feelings were at the moment may more easily be imagined than described,' Scott was to recall.

> After five months' imprisonment I was once more free, and in the hands of my own countrymen. I was penniless, and I might also say naked, for I knew that the clothes I had on would have to be thrown away; but I was going amongst Englishmen, and at that time no anxiety for the future troubled me.

Anne too had been awakened before dawn in her little room in Ningbo. Her attendant had come to her bedside saying 'Zhenhai, Chusan, get up!', and Bu Dingbang had called to her, confirming that she was indeed going to be leaving.

> Alas! poor fellow, he little thought that he was not to form one of the party, I am sure, you will believe me, when I tell you, that I knew not which thing to do first. Numbers of people came round my prison, and I was obliged to shut the door to keep them out. After my morning devotions, with the compradore's aid I got all my boxes packed. While thus engaged, he was sent for by the Mandarins, who told him, that he was not like the other English prisoners, they would therefore not allow him to accompany them, but send him down to Canton. This threw an immediate gloom over my spirits, and I felt deeply when, a few minutes afterwards, I saw him locked up in his prison, as he had long been my friend in adversity. I now with difficulty got through the crowd to the Gentlemen's prison, where I received

a hearty welcome and the warmest congratulations, and was forbidden to speak of past troubles. Captain Anstruther now insisted upon seeing the compradore to give him money, and, after many entreaties made to the Mandarin, whom he had greatly offended by withholding a picture for some unkindness shewn, he at last succeeded in beating his way through the crowd. We walked a great while in the prison yard until, by dint of perseverance and much pushing among the immense crowd, we got into our palanqueens. We had a guard to escort us, and, having crossed the river in our conveyances, I looked back and was astounded at the dense mass of spectators. Mandarins of every grade were in attendance. Indeed the excitement at Ningpo was indescribable. Our road to Chinhae [Zhenhai] led principally along the river side, and our travelling was anything but comfortable, the pass being so bad, that I feared our palanqueen bearers would slip. When near Chinhae, one of my bearers tumbled, and the palanqueen thumped on the ground. I struck my head, but the alarm was more than the injury. I thought my troubles would not be at an end, until I reached Chinhae. On the road we met several emissaries urging on the bearers to use all speed, to the mutual gratification of both parties. At last we arrived safely at Chinhae, where we were received with due honor by the Mandarins. We had not breakfasted, and, when the gentlemen asked for food, a filthy fellow came in with an apron full of cakes. Afterwards they brought us each a bason of meat. Captain Anstruther was now taken to see Commissioner E [i.e. Yilibu], and, after remaining a little while, he returned telling us, that we should soon be sent for to hear the same story told him, namely,—that we should not have come to China if the Admiral had not sent us, and that we must now

A sedan chair carrying one of the prisoners to Zhenhai (from Scott's *Narrative*).

return and tell the commanding officer, he must get the ships away with all speed, and, with his compliments say, that a great many soldiers were waiting to enter Chusan as soon as the English evacuated it, but, at the same time, he entreated us to labour under no apprehensions, for they had no hostile intentions. At first it was concluded, that Lieut. Douglas was to accompany me to Chusan, while Captain Anstruther should remain and see all the men embark; but, when we were with [Yilibu], Lieutenant Douglas told him, that Captain Anstruther had nothing to do with the people, and begged that he might be allowed to remain with his crew, and that Captain Anstruther might accompany me. It was at length determined, that both the gentlemen should stay behind, and only Mr. Witts accompany me. I made every inquiry for my only bonnet and other things, which the Mandarin had previously sent for to inspect, but in vain, as the officer had kept them and would not restore the same. Soon after, I took leave of the gentlemen and reentered my palanqueen which conveyed me to the waterside, where the linguist presented me with a fan. On the Mandarin's premises I had the pleasure of meeting all my fellow prisoners, which relieved my mind, as I was not before aware that they had come down from Ningpo, and had not seen them for several months. I spoke a few words to them as my sedan passed. On our way we were taken to the soldiers' tents; it being a late hour, and quite dark, I could see but little of them, but they appeared to be numerous and occupied a very large space. Every attention was now shewn me; they carried me close to the boatside and fixed a chair in the sampan for my comfort. The Mandarin who accompanied me, shewed me every attention.

For some hours our boat lay at anchor, to enable the other prisoners to embark, and during the night proceeded on her way to Chusan. About seven o'clock in the morning of the 26th [sic—it was the 24th], I was once more gladdened by the sight of an English vessel. Soon after, we were boarded by two naval officers and Mr. Johnson was the first to welcome me to freedom. In a short space of time, we saw several other vessels which lay at the outer anchorage; a few moments more, and the whole fleet was before us. I thought I saw as great a change on Chusan as on myself; the tents were no longer on the hills and to me, at least, all things looked strange, but perhaps the alteration was in me alone. As the boat drew near, Captain Bourchier of the *Blonde* sent his gig to convey me on board, and glad indeed was I to step into it, and thus quit for ever a people, at whose hands I had received such bitter wrongs. When safely arrived on the deck of the *Blonde*, I received the warmest congratulations of Captain Bourchier and the many friends to whom I was then introduced. What my feelings were at that time none but one so long in captivity can conceive. Every one seemed a participator in my enjoyment and each countenance wore the smile of heartfelt sympathy. I once more sat down to a comfortable breakfast, but my joy was too exquisite to allow me to partake. I remained on board the *Blonde* until the arrival of my fellow prisoners, whom I was most anxious to see once more. Lieutenant Douglas and Captain Anstruther soon joined us, and it heightened my pleasure greatly to see those, I so much esteemed, restored to their usual comforts and warm friends. Ere long, the European part of the crew came safely on board. I was much distressed at seeing their wasted frames and pale countenances, yet it was a cheering certainty that every kindness would now be shown them. It is to be hoped that, by the blessing of God, they will soon regain their wonted strength, and, I trust, the sad lesson they so dearly learned will never be erased from their memories.

Being most anxious to see you, my dear friend, and, Dr. Lockhart being in waiting to accompany me, I lost no time in hastening to the ship *Blundell*, where you had so carefully provided for my comfort. My dear friend Lieut. Douglas did not leave me, until I was safely on board; and no sooner had I reached the deck, than I received the loud and hearty cheers of the whole crew, which not being anticipated was completely overwhelming, combined as it was with the cordial welcome of Captain Trail and his officers. To describe our meeting would be needless—it is too indelibly engraven on the heart of each ever to be forgotten; but I would not conclude without a sincere, solemn, and heartfelt ascription of praise and thanks to the Almighty Father, the Gracious Saviour and the all-sustaining Spirit, who has so truly fulfilled his promise, 'I will not leave thee, nor forsake thee.'

And so, with a sentiment that encapsulated the faith that had sustained her over five long months, ended Anne's long letter to Mrs Gutzlaff.

8

'glad to be free of her cage'

THE ship *Blundell*, like the *Kite*, was a merchantman that had been requisitioned by the Royal Navy to transport materiel for the war in China. Her accommodation, so an advertisement in the *Sydney Morning Herald* promised, was 'very superior' for its day, and she was bound for the Portuguese territory of Macau, where Anne could recuperate before finding a vessel bound for England.

Already aboard the *Blundell* were Anne's friend and correspondent Mrs Mary Gutzlaff and her missionary husband Karl, Mary's teenage cousins Catherine and Isabella Parkes, and two blind Chinese girls—seven-year-old Laura, and five-year-old Agnes—whom the Gutzlaffs had adopted in Macau, taught English, and converted to Christianity. (Catherine and Isabella had arrived in China two years previously, sent there from their home in Bloxwich, Staffordshire, to join cousin Mary after their father's death had left them orphaned. They had been at her side ever since, arriving on Chusan after its capture by the British.) Dr William Lockhart too was aboard: he had closed his mission hospital in Dinghai only the day before. Mrs Noble, he wrote in a letter to the London Mission Society, 'now rejoices in her liberty, and expresses constant thankfulness to the Giver of all good for his mercy'.[1] Even the most faithful Christian would find it hard to imagine how she was able to thank God for his mercy after everything she had suffered.

By the time the *Blundell* dropped anchor in Macau a week or so later, Anne had finished composing her account of her experiences and had handed it to Mary Gutzlaff. Before the month of March was out, it had been published (with, we must assume given Mary's upright character, Anne's permission) as *A Narrative of the shipwreck of the Kite and of the imprisonment and sufferings of the crew and passengers in a letter from Mrs Anne Noble to a friend.*

The tiny peninsula of Macau—it was two miles long and just 500 yards wide at its waist—had been under Portuguese administration since the late sixteenth century. In 1841, with Hong Kong not yet ceded to the British, it was still the most important foreign foothold in China and a thoroughly European-looking town whose grandest buildings would not have looked out of place in Lisbon. Anne disembarked from the *Blundell* and was presumably found lodgings ashore, though where exactly we can't say: there were plenty of hotels in Macau to cater for a constant stream of merchants and missionaries, of soldiers and sailors and fortune-seekers, many of whom had their wives and families in tow. But Anne was possibly taken in as a private guest by a foreign resident: she had arrived under the care of Dr Lockhart, who had spent time at the Medical Missionary Society's hospital in Macau before sailing to Chusan and who still had many friends there; one of them was Benjamin Hobson, whose wife Jane now met with Anne and later corresponded with her.[2] Also on the *Blundell* had been Karl and Mary Gutzlaff, both of whom were extremely well placed within missionary, military, and governmental circles to seek out the most comfortable of accommodation.

Arriving with no little publicity and in such august company, Anne would have discovered that news of the *Kite*'s sinking and of her imprisonment had made

her something of a celebrity amongst the large foreign
community residing on the Pearl River delta. The chief
officer of the opium schooner *Black Joke* wrote to his father
in Suffolk, indignant at how she had been put into a wooden
cage 'and carried about some of the principal towns as a
show, and poked with iron pikes, as a butcher would a pig
or a bullock at home'.[3] Given the immense public sympathy
for Anne, not to mention the fact that she was still to all
intents and purposes destitute—she had said as much to
Lieutenant Douglas in one of her notes to him in Ningbo
gaol—it is unsurprising that a subscription was opened to
fund her stay in Macau and her passage home. No less a
man than Sir Humphrey Le Fleming Senhouse, second-
in-command of Britain's naval forces in China, wrote to
the fund's administrators in Macau 'under feelings of the
deepest indignation at the barbarous and savage conduct
of the Chinese'.

> I beg you will set my name down as a subscriber of £5
> to aid in procuring for Mrs. Noble the little comforts
> she must require in her desolate and pitiable state, as
> my mite, if she will condescend to accept the same,
> with whatever more may be added by others.[4]

Anne, Sir Humphrey noted, had been kept in prison 'until
the very moment almost in which she was about to bring
into the world an orphan child of her departed husband'. A
correspondent of *The New York Express* who was in Macau
at the same time as Anne wrote to that newspaper that
she had been 'far advanced in pregnancy' when she was
captured and put in her cage. So what happened to the baby
she had been carrying throughout her time in Ningbo?

Macau was certainly the best place in China for a
Western woman to give birth. In what must have made
for the starkest of contrasts with a Ningbo gaol, there was

no lack of excellent medical facilities: the Scottish surgeon Thomas Colledge had founded his ophthalmic hospital there two decades earlier, and the Medical Missionary Society had opened its own hospital in 1838. And far older than either of these were the Roman Catholics' Santa Casa da Misericóridia and the Hospital de São Rafael, both of which had been founded in the 1500s. If Dr Lockhart's calculations were correct, based on the letters she had sent Mrs Gutzlaff, then Anne would have been heavily pregnant in March of 1841 and due to give birth sometime in April. 'Mrs Noble is well and daily expects to be confined,' he was duly able to confirm on April 15th in a letter to his father and sister.[5] Four days later, it looked as if the child was still expected any day: 'Mrs Noble is well and I hope will soon be confined'.[6] Another four days passed, and Anne had still not given birth: 'Capt Elliott is at present in Macao, he is soon going over to Hongkong for a few days, when Mrs Noble has her confinement'.[7] Yet still the days passed and Mrs Noble did not go into labour.

It's not as though Anne had never experienced pregnancy before: she had given birth twice—once in Tyneside and once on board a ship. And Dr Lockhart, an experienced surgeon, must have been quite convinced of her condition: he had welcomed her aboard the *Blundell* when she first arrived back at Chusan after her release, and must have examined and quizzed her as to her health. They had sailed to Macau together on the same ship. And so he—and indeed Anne—must have been thoroughly bemused when, sometime during April or May, she realised that she not been pregnant after all. He next mentioned the matter in a letter of June 1st:

> Mrs Noble of whom I have often spoken is about to proceed home at once. I said in a former letter that she expected to be confined shortly and from what

she told me I thought this would be the case but on
further enquiry lately I found it was not so and she
therefore is about to leave for England at once.

'Mrs Noble is about to go to England in the *Apolline* to
London,' he finally confirmed three weeks later. 'I think I
told you her supposed pregnancy was a mistake altogether.'[8]
Even before her imprisonment, Anne had been of slight
build—Edward Cree had described her as 'raw-boned'
after meeting her in Trincomalee. Then there had been the
indescribable torment of bereavement, days at sea, capture,
and beatings, followed by weeks of confinement in a tiny
cage and an inadequate diet. It would be no surprise if
she had miscarried during the first trimester—this might
explain the violent pains of October—and had not started
to menstruate again until weeks after her release. It might
even have been that the psychological blow of bereavement
led to a full-blown 'phantom pregnancy', with Anne
grieving so deeply for her baby and its father that her mind
and body played tricks on her and she and her doctors
came to believe that she was again carrying James's child.

It is impossible to say whether Anne felt relieved to be
spared the pain of childbirth or distraught at not having
the baby which had been fathered by the man she loved.
But while Dr Lockhart had reported that Anne was well,
the chief officer of the *Black Joke* disagreed: Anne, he wrote,
was still 'suffering most acutely from her late cruel usage,
as also from the loss of her husband and child.'[9]

In little more than a month, more than $8,000 had been
raised for Anne among the British community on the
China coast. After a ticket for her voyage home had been
procured and the silver dollars converted into pounds
sterling, there was the very substantial sum of £2,030 to
be remitted to London for investment in government
bonds.[10] A few days before her departure, Anne wrote to

the trustees of her subscription fund—James Matheson, Lancelot Dent, and Thomas Gibb—to thank them;[11] it is the only letter of hers we have other than that which she wrote to Mrs Gutzlaff. There is no hint that she bore any ill-will against these three merchants, whose trading in opium had after all been the ultimate cause of the war that had claimed her husband and son.

> Gentlemen,
>
> To you in particular, as well as my kind friends in general, I would, ere I leave Macao, offer my deepest gratitude for the very liberal subscription raised on my behalf in my affliction; and the rich provision made for myself and beloved child [i.e., Annie, in North Shields]. Your generous efforts and warm sympathy can only be duly felt and appreciated by one so bitterly afflicted, bereaved, and so truly destitute as myself. But my heart can take pleasure in the universally kind feeling evinced towards me; surely, you have caused the heart of the widow to rejoice, and the god of the fatherless shall bless you. Yes, we have the firm promise of the Almighty that you shall be rewarded. Will you, gentlemen, oblige me by transmitting these my sentiments to my numerous friends. Permit me to remain with gratitude, yours ever indebted,
>
> Anne Noble.

On July 17th, Anne sailed for London upon the *Apolline*,[12] a 'splendid new coppered and copper-fastened barque' which boasted 'very superior accommodation for a few respectable cabin passengers'.[13] In Anne's care were Laura and Agnes, the two blind Chinese girls; and in the *Apolline*'s hold was a cargo of teas—pekoe, congou, twankay and young hyson[14]—that expensive commodity, the high demand for which in Britain was the counterpart to the illegal opium trade on the China coast. The *Apolline* called at St Helena,[15] where her passengers must have been disappointed to discover that the island's most famous former resident, Napoleon Bonaparte, had only a few months previously been disinterred from his resting place of twenty years and taken back to Paris for reburial. All in all, then, the voyage was a rather apt distillation of the times.

The ship reached London on December 29th, 1841,[16] and Anne seems to have lost no time in returning to North Shields and her sister-in-law Isabella,† where she was reunited with the daughter she had not seen for two and a half years. She must have been longing to pass the time quietly with her Annie, but she instead discovered that she had become something of a celebrity at home as well as in China.

At a time when even the daguerrotype was in its infancy, the likenesses of the famous (and the infamous) could only be mass-produced and disseminated using engravings taken from sketches or paintings, but it just so happened that Anne's return to England coincided with advances in printing technology and the advent of the world's first pictorial newspaper. The *Illustrated London News* had been appearing for less than three months when it carried a rather fanciful image of Mrs Noble, her hair nicely dressed and wearing a voluminous gown, sitting upright in the cage while her Chinese visitors inspected her.[17] And Anne

† The 1841 Census records Isabella and Annie living in George Street. Two letters in Anne's correspondence from 1842 are addressed to her at No. 16, so it is clear that she was living there during this time. The brick terraces of George Street have since been demolished (many were damaged during the Blitz) and replaced by a council estate and industrial units.

'A Chinese Cage' (*Illustrated London News*, September 13th, 1842).

had only been back a few weeks when she was approached
by a lady artist who asked to paint her portrait, hoping
presumably to make from it a print which could be more
widely sold.[18] Anne wrote to a friend in London asking for
advice, and was told that it was impertinent of any artist to
ask such a thing of a total stranger. A church service was
the most likely place for other artists to attempt to make a
sketch of her likeness, she was warned, and she was advised
to frustrate them by keeping her black mourning veil over
her face when in public.[19] Anne was also reminded that
people might try to print and sell copies of her *Narrative
of the Shipwreck of the Kite* without her permission—if
she found any such copies on sale, she should have her
solicitor take legal action against the publisher. Rather
sadly, her desire for privacy means that no known portrait
has survived beyond the tiny sketch by Edward Cree of a
redheaded Anne looking forlorn in her cage.

Neither did Anne find peace of mind in her old home,
where reminders of her life before she and James sailed for
China were all around. A letter she received in the spring
of 1842 from a 'Mrs Lingham'[†] refers to the tenor of a letter

which Anne had earlier written, in which she clearly struck Mrs Lingham as unhappy: North Shields, it was apparent to her, offered no consolation as a place where Anne might usefully mourn her loss. Still, Mrs Lingham assured her, their Heavenly Father would reconcile her to her home in North Shields if it was His will that she should be there.

At least Anne no longer needed to fear destitution, given that she now had some £2,000 to her name. Another financial matter was that of the money owed to her as the widow of a man who had died while in the service of the Royal Navy. Soon after returning home, she applied to the Admiralty for the arrears of almost £26 that were due to her and discovered that her ordeal in China had won her some very influential supporters.[20] Mrs Lingham, clearly a very well-connected woman, helped Anne by volunteering as a go-between. Besides meeting with Alderman John Pirie the Lord Mayor of London, Mrs Lingham enlisted the help of the famous arctic explorer Sir William Edward Parry, who as the Royal Navy's Comptroller of Steam Machinery had clout within the Admiralty. Parry encouraged Mrs Lingham to write to the prime minister Sir Robert Peel. This she did, also using her contacts within the Royal Household to meet with Major-General Sir Henry Wheatley, Keeper of the Privy Purse, and to win assurances that Anne's case would be brought directly to the attention of Her Majesty Queen Adelaide, widow of the late King William IV. In September of 1841, Lord Palmerston, who as foreign secretary had launched the war against China, had even raised her name in the House of Commons when

† 'Mrs Lingham' of 34, Great St. Helen's, might have been related to the Thomas Lingham of no. 35, who in 1846 is named as a subscriber to *The Beauties of the Holy Bible*. Nothing more has been discovered about either person.

haranguing Prime Minister Robert Peel. (Yes, Mrs Noble had suffered barbarous ill-usage, Palmerston mocked, but still the contents of a personal letter to her from Captain Senhouse were no foundation upon which the nation's finances could be decided!)[21] For the daughter of a Wiltshire millworker to be known by name in such circles, and even to be looked upon as a friend by some, was quite remarkable.

Though Anne was now living in relative seclusion half a world away, her release from gaol in February of 1841 and the subsequent evacuation of British troops from Chusan had not brought the war in China to an end. Instead of peace, the fighting had quickly flared up again at the mouth of the Pearl River outside Canton, and in October of that same year—while Anne was sailing back to England upon the *Apolline*—Chusan had been attacked and captured for a second time. A particularly cold winter in Zhejiang had forced both sides to call a temporary halt to their plans, but spring of 1842 had seen the conflict erupt once more and by the summer it had reached a crescendo. With a flotilla of British warships blockading the Yangtze and threatening to bombard China's second city, the emperor's commissioners (among them the elderly Yilibu, who had freed Anne and the other prisoners) agreed to the terms of the Treaty of Nanjing: China would pay reparations of $21,000,000, Hong Kong island would be ceded to the Crown, and ports including Shanghai and Ningbo would be thrown open to British merchants. News of the peace reached England in time for the *Argus* to include it in its annual 'Nonsense for New Year's Day', a satirical round-up of the year's events which dragged on for eighty-one lines of the laziest rhymes imaginable: [22]

'glad to be free of her cage'

The Chinese, as you know, have been ordered to run
To their tills, and to shell out their tin by the ton,
And we'll bet twenty pounds to a stale Sally Lunn,
That they're sick of the sound of an islander's gun.
And so they're allowed our ball practice to shun,
They'll fill with their dollars the Heidelburg tun.[†]

Miss Kemble has left (for the present) the stage,
Duke Brunswick has ventured to law with the *Age*.
The Cardinal's now with the ladies the rage,
Mr Dickens's 'notes' are more slip-slop than sage.
In the *Wives*, we've Miss Poole as the pretty Miss Page.
Mrs Noble is glad to be free of her cage.

Though with the exception of Charles Dickens their names
have all now faded into obscurity, the author of the *Argus*'s
Nonsense was able to mention Anne alongside some of the
best-known personages of the day: Miss Adelaide Kemble
was an opera singer from a family of celebrated performers;
Charles II, Duke of Brunswick, had been ousted from his
dukedom and was suing *The Age*, a satirical paper with a
reputation for extorting money from society figures; 'The
Cardinal' was a role then being played by the dashing Mr
Tilbury at the Theatre Royal, Haymarket; Miss Eliza Poole
was a popular actress who had first taken to the stage at the
age of seven and was at the time playing Anne Page in *The
Merry Wives of Windsor* at London's Covent Garden.

Besides word of the terms of the Nanjing treaty, there
was another reason why the late hostilities in China—and
Anne's name in particular—were in the news at this time,
for in late July of 1842 an unexpected reminder of Anne's
imprisonment had surfaced. HMS *Wellesley* had arrived

---

† An *extraordinarily* large wine barrel in Heidelberg Castle, capable of
holding some 219,000 litres (though now regrettably empty).

in Plymouth bearing curiosities from the Orient—there was an anchor so rudely constructed that surprise was expressed at how poor the Chinese were at ironwork—and war trophies brought back by the ship's crew (though these were promptly confiscated by customs officers to the great chagrin of the press). Of more interest to the public, though, was the very same cage in which Anne had been held. Accurately measured now, its dimensions were shocking:

> To give some idea of the state of torture to which the English are subjected by the august relatives of the Sun and the Moon, we give the description of this instrument. It is made of rough fir stakes; and measures only two feet eight inches in length, one foot six inches in breadth, and two feet four inches in depth, with a hole on the top for the unfortunate lady's head to come through; so that when the head protruded the inmate could neither sit nor stand upright.[23]

One wooden cage might look very much like the next, but there was no doubt that this was the genuine article. After recapturing Chusan in October of 1841, the British had pressed home their advantage by taking Ningbo without a shot needing to be fired. Philip Anstruther (promoted to the rank of major since his release) had led the Madras Artillery into the city and found himself billeted at first in the residence of the *taidao*, the self-same building that housed his and Anne's former gaol.[24] There he had returned favours to the old turnkeys who had been kind to him, and had liberated his own cage, Anne's cage, and also the iron shackles he had been made to wear.[25] But, being sited as it was near the heart of the city, the *taidao*'s residence was soon abandoned as a billet and condemned as the fuel store for the winter, (a few old bricks, a little wood, and half-a-dozen old Chinese matchlocks made up an excellent grate in half-an-hour), and long before the cold season had passed, its beams, rafters, doors, and windows had been consigned to the fire-places of the barrack-rooms, and nothing but the ruined walls of the capacious building remained.[26]

Anne's cage meanwhile had been placed in a crate and loaded onto the *Wellesley* for the voyage home. Reaching Plymouth, it had been taken by paddle-steamer to London's Woolwich Dockyard to be delivered to the United Service Club in Pall Mall, care of Captain Thomas Maitland, who had commanded the Wellesley in China.[27] Captain Maitland donated Anne's cage to the United Service Museum in Great Scotland Yard, where it joined curiosities such as Captain Cook's chronometer and Sir Francis Drake's walking stick. Though Anne herself had been freed from captivity more than two years earlier, her cage itself now achieved something of a celebrity status and propelled her back into the public's consciousness. Now a permanent exhibit, and surrounded by military memorabilia (there were captured Turkish *yataghans*, Gurkha knives, Oliver Cromwell's sword, a cannon from the *Mary Rose*, French and Chinese battle standards, even the skeleton of Napoleon Bonaparte's favourite horse, Marengo), it was viewed by thousands of visitors.[28] An engraving of the cage standing amongst the museum's other exhibits was printed in *The Pictorial Times*, and newspapers from Cornwall to Edinburgh and from Suffolk to Dublin carried its description: it was 'so small that the unfortunate captive must have remained during the whole time in a crouching position.' It would be fair to say that there could scarcely have been a soul in the United Kingdom who was not familiar with the name Anne Noble and the story of her dastardly imprisonment. And remarkably, given how deeply she had suffered in China, just a few weeks after her cage had arrived in England even Anne herself once again set eyes on it, only this time as guest of the museum's secretary.[29] By now she had left behind North Shields and the memories it held for her, and was living in Doddington Grove, Kennington[30]—'a quiet, wide and pleasant avenue of plane trees and cottages'[31]—possibly with a wine merchant by the name of George Sievers, and his wife.[32] (As James Noble had carried cargoes of wine from France to Mauritius, it is possible that Sievers was an old business associate).

Given the Victorians' love of inspiring the next generation of empire-builders, it is unsurprising that a children's version of Anne's story very soon found its way onto the nation's bookshelves. *The Recreation*, published in 1843, was 'a gift-book for young readers, embracing such subjects as are particularly fitted to interest and improve the youthful mind'. It contained all manner of what were no doubt fascinating topics to children of the day, such as buffalo hunting on the North American prairies, the great fire of Hamburg, anecdotes of the spotted flycatcher, the death of Ali Pasha, and the suppression of the Janissaries. But *The Recreation* also contained Anne and Anstruther's letters and excerpts from Scott's lengthy *Narrative*, with no attempt at sanitising the horrors of disease, violence, and death.

Public interest in Anne's story must still have been going strong when on Boxing Day of 1845 the 'Nobility, Clergy, Gentry, and the Inhabitants of Bristol and its Vicinity'[33] were invited to witness

GOMPERTZ's New and Magnificent PANORAMA, ILLUSTRATING, IN THIRTEEN VIEWS, the principal events connected with THE WAR WITH CHINA

At a time when photography was in its infancy and accounts of major events were only rarely illustrated, audiences flocked to see colourful dioramas that brought global events to life. In Bristol's Assembly Rooms, painted scenes from the recent Opium War were presented to adults and children alike to the accompaniment of a brass band.[34] Each act would already have been familiar from newspaper accounts: here was the walled city of Canton the audience had read so much about, the fleet of Chinese war-junks (one of these was somehow made to explode!), the island of Hong Kong which had been won for Queen Victoria, the 'Terrific Descent of the Burning Rafts at Midnight', the British bombardment of Amoy, and more. Finally came 'The City of Ningpo, and Cage with Mrs Noble'.[35] Mr Gompertz's panorama proved so popular that on its final night three months later an extra performance had to be added to avoid overcrowding. The show decamped to Bath, then to Reading, then to Southampton, then to more than a dozen other towns and cities across the south of England,[†] and even to the Channel Islands.[36] Everywhere it went, it was received with rapturous applause: 'We had heard much of this far-famed work of art,' wrote one spectator,

> which so happily blends solid historical fact and valuable collateral information with pure unalloyed

---

† These included Salisbury, Winchester, Portsea, Exeter, Plymouth, Devonport, Truro, Penzance, Falmouth, Redruth, and Torquay.

intellectual amusement. It is a masterly production, and has gained the admiration of all who have seen it.[37]

Mr Gompertz's scenes from the Opium War were still being performed in 1850, nine years after Anne had been freed, though by then they were but a small part of an evening's entertainment which had grown to encompass the Invasion of British India by the Seikh Army of the Punjaub (this spectacle topped the bill), the Crypt of the Holy Sepulchre in Jerusalem, and the Great Fire of London. Then in 1851, Mr Gompertz began exhibiting a new set of panoramas, based on the exploration of the Canadian arctic and the search for Sir John Franklin. Perhaps he had grown jaded after five years of presenting the same show every night; or perhaps his grand dioramas had become worn out through overuse. Anne's remained a household name, but she had gone from being the object of outpourings of genuine sympathy to an image from yesteryear's news painted upon a fading canvas.

On the other side of the globe, though, far from being forgotten, Anne was being remembered—but as a *very* different person. The Japanese were intensely interested in what was becoming of China. For centuries they had looked with admiration across the sea to a culture which had massively influenced their own, and they had watched with apprehension at displays of Britain's military power; Chusan was, after all, less than 500 miles from the Japanese mainland.

In 1843, a scholar named Saito Chikudo had written an early account of the Opium War, based on reports brought to Japan by merchants who had learned of the events.[38] On the 20th day of the 9th lunar month, he said,

> a foreign ship arrived off Yuyao county, Ningbo. The local population hurriedly gathered to repulse it, but the foreigners, ignorant of the geography of the area, accidentally ran aground on a shoal and could not get their ship off. On board were huge cannons, whose booming was like an earthquake, and their firing caused the ship to break apart. When the locals boarded the ship, the foreigners put to sea in small boats and fled, but they captured a female chieftain and twenty of her followers. Her bravery was exceptional, and she killed five or six men, breaking dozens of swords and guns. The Chinese were routed, but one man attacked her from behind, brandishing a gun. The female chieftain was by now exhausted, and she was captured by the throng. They called her the Third Princess of the English. (In England there are three such women; one is the present ruler and another is a vice-general, and these two are both in England.) The third is an admiral, and this is the woman who was captured. She was bright of eye and had beautiful brows, with lustrous black hair and snow-white skin. She was around eighteen years old, and resembled an oriental woman.[39]

Saito's depiction of Anne is so utterly at odds with reality that we have almost to consciously remind ourselves that this is the very same woman! Six years later, a different Japanese scholar wrote *New Stories from Overseas*, a detailed and vivid (though not wholly accurate) account of the war.[40] Unfortunately for its author, Mineta Fuko, its potential for alarming the Japanese public with its depiction of the British threat led to the book being suppressed by the authorities. Mineta Fuko and the book's

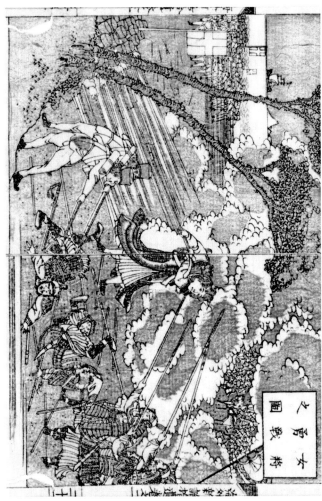

'Woman warrior bravely fighting,' a woodblock illustration from *Gleanings from 'New Stories from Overseas'*, depicts Anne Noble as a princess leading her troops against the Chinese (reproduced from an original copy, with the kind permission of Victor Schenk).

illustrator were both imprisoned (the illustrator died in gaol) and the wooden print-blocks were burned. Before Mineta could be captured, though, he had been daring enough to publish a sequel, *Gleanings from 'New Stories from Overseas'*.[41] Mineta had added to his earlier work by including—and massively over-embellishing—the story of Anne Noble, the 'female chieftain', even giving her magical powers.[42] One of Mineta's marvellous woodblock illustrations—'Woman warrior bravely fighting'—shows Anne leading the British troops against the Chinese, who fall to the ground beneath the onslaught!

But Anne could not possibly have known of her transformation from a bedraggled widow in a cage to a warrior princess; and even if a woodblock print of Mineta's *Gleanings* had by some miracle found its way to England, Anne had in any case long since sailed for the United States.

9

item no. 2674

IN THE summer of 1844, Anne and her daughter Annie travelled the few miles upriver from their home in North Shields to the Newcastle waterfront. There they boarded the ship *Normandie*, which arrived in New York on September 20th. (Sadly, after the *Normandie* left New York for Hull deeply laden with bales of cotton, she was caught in a winter storm and went down with all hands. Such were the real risks of ocean voyaging in the romantic age of sail.)[1] We do not know what precisely motivated Anne to emigrate at this point, though she must have had fond memories of her time in New York more than a decade earlier—this was, after all, the city where she and her late husband had met, briefly courted, and married. In England, she would forever be remembered as the poor Mrs Noble who had been so cruelly mistreated by the Chinese; the United States had not been involved in the Opium War, and though American newspapers had reported her story she was not nearly so well known and could start a new life. More pertinently, several of Anne's immediate family from Trowbridge were already settled in New York: her elder brother James, who had been living in the city when Anne visited in 1833, had since married a local woman and by 1844 was the father of five children. Anne's youngest sibling Benjamin too might already have been there by this time, as he was certainly living in James' home by 1850; but it was with her younger brother Henry that she and Annie settled in Brooklyn. Four years later, in 1848, Anne and her brothers were joined there by their elderly mother Susannah and sister Olivia. Olivia had married an English merchant named Thomas Reynolds and borne a child to him, and the extended family began living together in Thomas's house, which seems to have stood on the corner of Clinton Avenue and Fulton Street.[2] Anne returned to England on just one occasion, it appears, for in 1859 we find her and Annie, by then a grown woman of twenty-one, leaving London and crossing the Atlantic for the last time aboard the *American Eagle*. The fact that they occupied the first cabin on the ship's manifest is an indication that they were still comfortably well off.

Given the intensely devout Christian faith that comes across so strongly in Anne's *Narrative*, it is hardly surprising that she and her daughter became active congregants of Plymouth Church in Brooklyn Heights. Its pastor was the outspoken abolitionist Henry Ward Beecher (brother of Harriet Beecher Stowe, author of *Uncle Tom's Cabin*), who in the years leading up to the US Civil War filled the pews with his powerful preaching and mock slave-auctions. Anne and Annie were in the habit of sitting in the front row to hear Henry's sermons, and he became a personal friend: 'Your Mr Beecher' (as Annie's friends would always teasingly refer to him) was in the habit of walking the two women home after services and joining them for Sunday lunch.

Anne and Annie lived in Brooklyn throughout the Civil War. Neither that city nor its twin, New York, which faced it across the East River, sat directly in the path of the two armies as they clashed. The so-called 'high water mark' of the Confederate forces—the furthest point to which they advanced within Union territory—was Gettysburg, still a 200-mile march short of Brooklyn. The most serious fighting to take place in the state of New York during the war was in fact the Draft Riots of 1863, four days of bloodshed sparked by discontent among working-class Irish immigrants at new laws conscripting them into the Union Army (the 2002 film *Gangs of New York* dramatizes some of the events). Beyond this, the only damage done by the war which any of the Nobles or the Watsons might have set eyes upon was that caused by a gang of Confederate agents who in 1864 started a number of fires in Manhattan in the hope of causing a major conflagration.

Annie herself, though, was affected in a very personal way by the war. In her early twenties she had become close to a man named Otis Moody, who shared her evangelical Protestant convictions and her opposition to slavery. Otis enlisted in the 51st Illinois Volunteers shortly after the start of the war in 1861 but continued to woo Annie in his letters.[3] After he was mortally wounded at the Battle of Chickamauga two years later, she learned that he had left his New Testament to her in his will. Five years after this earnest suitor's death, and with encouragement from her aunt and confidante, Anne's younger sister Olivia, in 1868 Annie married the luxuriantly named Charles Eliphalet Walbridge, a retired lieutenant-colonel and Civil War veteran. Charles hailed from the city of Buffalo in upstate New York, and it was decided that they would set up home there and that Anne (by now 54 years of age) would live with them.

Buffalo—'the Queen City of the Lakes'—was at the time, as the western terminus of the Erie Canal, one of the fastest-growing and most prosperous cities in the US: the completion of the canal in 1825 had allowed ships to sail from the Atlantic Ocean into the Great Lakes, opening up America's West to new settlement and providing a route by which the agricultural products of the Midwest could be transported to the densely populated Eastern Seaboard. When Anne and her daughter left Brooklyn for their new home, Buffalo was already a vital link in the chain that carried wheat from the prairies to New England and onward to Europe. The city was then the world's largest supplier of grain, with vast quantities arriving by ship from Michigan, Illinois and elsewhere to be transferred to the enormous grain elevators that dominated the lakeshore. With the increase in trade came railroads and migrants, and as Buffalo's population soared so did the demand for goods and services. Charles, who had worked for a hardware dealer before the Civil War, opened his own store in downtown Buffalo. The business boomed, and the Walbridges moved into the smart, new Italianate house at No. 142, Cottage Street.[4]

Precisely how Anne Noble passed her final years we cannot say—we know less about her life in Buffalo than we do about the few turbulent months she spent in China. Given what we know of her religious faith she must have been active in her local Christian community, and she appears to have attended the North Presbyterian Church, a mile from the Walbridges' home:[†] her daughter Annie's father-in-law, George B. Walbridge, had been one of that church's three founding elders in 1846, and Annie's husband Charles led the Sunday school there during the years that Anne was living with them.[5]

Anne must surely have ridden the railroad north to see one of the world's great natural wonders; and there, watching the Niagara River cascade with such immense

[†] The church then stood on Main Street (its site is now Fountain Plaza). In 1906, the congregation moved into a newly built church on Delaware Ave and Utica Street (which is now Greek Orthodox).

force over the falls, she might have been reminded of the powerful tide that years before had stolen her husband away and drowned her infant son. She died at the age of 63, and was laid to rest in Forest Lawn Cemetery, three and a half thousand miles from her birthplace in Wiltshire and twice that distance from Ningbo. But she had never forgotten what happened to her in China: her granite headstone gives pride of place not to her, but to her late husband. It reads:

NOBLE
IN MEMORY OF
JAMES SMITH NOBLE R.N.
COMMANDER OF H.B.M. BRIG KITE
WHO WAS DROWNED IN THE WRECK
OF HIS SHIP OFF THE COAST OF CHINA
SEPT. 15, 1841
AND HIS WIFE
ANNE WATSON
WHO DIED AT THE HOME OF THEIR DAUGHTER
MRS. CHARLES E. WALBRIDGE IN BUFFALO
DEC. 28, 1877
ALSO OF THEIR INFANT SON
RALPH
WHO PERISHED WITH HIS FATHER
IN THE WRECK OF THE KITE

Reading the inscription closely, we might surmise that it was not Anne herself who dictated its wording, for there are several errors: Anne would have known that her husband James had never been in the Royal Navy, and that the *Kite* was not one of Her Britannic Majesty's brigs but instead a civilian merchant vessel; more importantly, that James and Ralph had drowned in 1840 rather than 1841 must have been seared onto her memory. Why then these basic mistakes? As Anne grew older, it's possible that she began to lose her mental acuity and that the facts of her life before moving to the US altered with each retelling. Perhaps she herself, thirty years and more later, misremembered her first and only husband as the commander of a Royal Naval brig; or, more likely, he was mistakenly given a posthumous commission by his daughter Annie and her husband Charles, who must so often have heard, repeated, and occasionally embellished the story. After all, none of Anne's family in Buffalo—even her daughter—had ever known James. It would be no surprise if Anne had kept September 15th, the anniversary of her sudden bereavement, as a day of solemn remembrance, but no surprise if Annie had forgotten which year *precisely* her mother was commemorating.

Annie Fenwick Walbridge (née Noble) bore five children to Charles and passed away in 1910. Both her sons died very soon after birth, and, alone out of her three daughters,

Anne's daughter, Annie Fenwick, photographed later in life.

her eldest child, Wilhelmina, married and had children. Wilhelmina herself died in 1950. The last of Anne Noble's six great-grandchildren passed away in 2004, having between them borne her six great-great-grandchildren, who bore ten great-great-great-grandchildren, and in turn sixteen great-great-great-great-grandchildren. Today they are spread across the Eastern seaboard of the United States, the country where a teenage dressmaker named Mary Anne Watson went to find work but instead fell in love with a sea captain.

Major Philip Anstruther went on to become an archetype of the British imperial soldier. For his military service in China, Queen Victoria appointed him a Companion of the Order of the Bath. Still only in his mid-thirties, Anstruther had already had enough adventures to fill a lifetime, but there were plenty yet to come. After another decade serving in India, during which time he fought in the Second Anglo-Sikh War in the Punjab, in 1851 he was granted overseas leave. Rather than return to Scotland, he sailed straight for Africa and the latest war which was then being fought between the settlers of the Cape Colony and the Xhosa to the east, and there he campaigned alongside the Cape Mounted Riflemen in the foothills of the Amatola Mountains. Not content with this, he then sailed across the Bay of Bengal to help out in the Second Anglo-Burmese War. But when in 1855 his elder brother died without an heir, Anstruther inherited the family estate in Fife,[6] and the following summer he arrived back on the P&O steamship *Pera* to take up his lairdship.[7] He retired in 1858 with the rank of Major-General, eventually published his *Theory of Gunnery* (which he had begun in chalk on the walls of his Ningbo cell), and died in 1884 at the age of 76.

Despite the passing of 43 years, his obituary in *The Times* still highlighted his time as a prisoner of the Chinese. He lies buried alongside his parents in the village kirkyard at Kilrenny. As for the cage in which he was imprisoned, he proudly took it back to India as a souvenir after the conclusion of the First Opium War, and it is still on public display in the museum at Fort St George, Madras.

Anstruther's family friend Lieutenant Charles Douglas returned to England and was promoted to the rank of naval commander. His care for the soldiers and sailors imprisoned with him in Ningbo had not been forgotten: 'His gallant conduct and noble self devotion on several occasions met with unqualified and universal approbation from the officers of our fleet at China'.[8] But despite his promotion and his aristocratic blood, Charles continued to suffer from the effects of his incarceration. When he married in the society church of St James, Westminster, he was already on half-pay, and soon afterwards he accepted a land-based posting with the coastguard in County Wexford.[9] He retired from this position after only five years, and died in London aged just 39.

Chief Officer Richard Witts fared even worse. He remained in China with the British expedition for a whole year after his release from gaol but then sailed for England. His death was announced in his local newspaper, *The Bury and Norwich Post*:

> Died. In the 32nd year of his age, on his passage home from China, Mr RG Witts, eldest son of Mrs Frances Witts, of Sepulchre Street, Sudbury. Mr Witts was chief officer of the *Kite*, when that vessel was wrecked on a quicksand on the Coast of China, on her voyage to Chusan.... The hardships and cruelties suffered by Mr Witts were so great that his constitution, naturally good, and seasoned by many years service in Tropical

climates, was so debilitated, that it was believed nothing but a return to his native country could restore him; his arrival was most anxiously expected by his disconsolate mother and family, but death put an end to his sufferings on the 17th of February last.[10]

Pellew Webb remained a sailor for more than two decades, but he too finally fell prey to the sea. In 1863 he was lost overboard from the passenger steamship *Australian* during a voyage from Burma to Calcutta, aged just 42. His friend Henry Twizell returned home to North Shields later than anticipated (he was left stranded in Macau after going ashore to buy clothes!) and also continued to earn a living as a sailor, eventually passing the exam to become a Master Mariner.[11] After a night of heavy drinking a decade later he found himself before a court for assaulting two policemen—possibly the strain of his imprisonment continued to prey on his mind.[12] He married,[13] but he too died young, at 48 years of age.

John Lee Scott, who left the most detailed record of events in Ningbo, was given passage home aboard HMS *Samarang* with his fellow apprentices from the *Kite* and arrived back in August of 1841. He must have spent the next three months writing, as his *Narrative of a Recent Imprisonment in China* was in print before November was out. It was given creditable reviews, which is unsurprising given that the British public had been following Anne's capture in the newspapers, even if they had not heard John's name. John's success contributed to Anne's fame but also went some way to painting a more vivid and complex portrait of the Chinese than the simplistic black and white terms in which accounts of the war had thus far been sketched. *Narrative of a Recent Imprisonment* sold well and went into a second edition the next year. John married in 1849 and spent the next decade living in a very well-to-do street in London's Bloomsbury. But from describing himself as a 'landed proprietor' in the 1850s, his fortunes faltered: a decade later, he was living in Gravesend as an agent to a dock company, and he spent the rest of his working life as a clerk. Yet unlike most of his fellow prisoners he seems to have remained healthy, fathering at least seven children and living to see the early years of the twentieth century.

Bu Dingbang, the Chinese compradore who had helped the British find provisions on Chusan, was beheaded on the orders of commissioner Yuqian not long after Anne and the others had been freed. The Qing dynasty's penal code imposed collective responsibility in serious criminal cases, including treason, and upon Bu's capture in 1840 his entire family—mother, father, wife, daughter, and three brothers—had also been gaoled and their property seized. His father and two brothers died in custody, and the others were only released in late 1842. With not a copper cash to their name Bu's entire extended family was homeless, though the British community in Canton agreed to support them.[14]

Laura and Agnes, the two blind Chinese girls whom Anne had accompanied to England on the *Apolline*, were delivered into the care of the London Society for Teaching the Blind to Read.[15] Taught to read using Lucas Type, a predecessor of braille, both seem to have flourished in London, becoming fluent in English and (unsurprisingly, given the religious nature of their adoption and schooling) piously Christian. Laura became a teacher at the school but died in 1854, and Agnes sailed back to China the following year. Thoroughly 'rescued from heathen wretchedness',[16] she began teaching at the School of Industry for the Blind in Ningbo, the very same city in which Anne Noble had been imprisoned. When in 1861 Ningbo was captured by the Taiping rebels, Agnes moved to Shanghai where she continued to teach the blind to read while giving English lessons—she spoke this better than her native language—to wealthy Chinese. She 'worked hard, lived sparingly and saved money', and at her death her property was left to found a modest hospital.[17] In escorting Agnes to England when the girl was barely five years old, Anne had played a role, if only a small one, in building a unique role model for the Chinese—a blind woman who used her foreign education to earn her way, live independently, and pass on those strengths to others like her.

Anne's cage, the subject of so many illustrations in the years after her capture, long remained in its room at the United Service Museum. In 1858 it was visited by Queen Victoria herself.[18] It was still on display in the 1920s (it shared space with relics of the recent Great War: parts of a German zeppelin, and a British 'flame gun')[19] and was listed in the museum's catalogue in 1932, but by the time the next inventory was taken in the 1950s it had disappeared. Many of the museum's holdings were sold off at one time or another, but no record was kept of where they went. As the decades passed, the story behind the brief description attached to Item No. 2674—(Noble, Mrs., Chinese Cage)—was forgotten. The cage presumably reverted to the workaday object its makers had intended, and was eventually thrown away as worthless.

Philip Anstruther never married, and on his death the iron handcuffs and shackles he had worn in Ningbo passed to a niece. This Miss Graham, perhaps bemused at inheriting such a strange souvenir, presented them to the Anstruther estate, where they were mounted and hung upon the wall. They are still there today, along with two very pleasing paintings by Philip himself of the artist being carried about in his tiny cage. As the years passed, his stories of kidnap and imprisonment became part of

Anstruther family legend, so much so that it was even suspected he had made them up. As is so often the case, the truth is far stranger than any tale he might have spun over drinks in the officers' mess.

Acknowledgments

My sincere thanks to everyone who has helped me to amass the primary sources that document Anne's life and times: to Molly Turlish and Buffie Kelly for their invaluable help regarding Anne's life and family in the US, and for tracking down and scanning the photograph of Annie Fenwick Walbridge (I would never have discovered the notes sent to Anne in Ningbo gaol without Molly's assistance); also in this regard to Ron O'Callaghan, who transcribed them some years back, and to the anonymous collector in whose possession the notes now are (having tried and failed to contact the collector (or even to discover their identity), I offer my sincerest apologies for referring to the content of the notes without their express permission and would be delighted to hear from them if ever they learn of this book); to Deborah Jamieson at the Balcaskie Estate in Fife for arranging for my wife and I to view Captain Anstruther's shackles and paintings and for driving us to see them; to Toby Anstruther for his kind permission to reproduce them in this book; to Victor Schenk, proud owner of a copy of *Gleanings from 'New Stories from Overseas'*, who very mindly provided me with the image of the woodblock illustration of Anne fighting the Chinese; to Laura Dimmock-Jones of RUSI, for endeavouring to track down what became of Anne's cage; and to Henrietta Heawood, present owner of Edward Cree's diaries.

Sources and Bibliography

(i) Printed works in English

The Blind and their Books; with some account of Laura Gutzlaff, a native of China (London, 1859).

The Female Missionary Intelligencer for 1857.

Fortieth Annual Report of the London Society for Teaching the Blind to Read (1878).

The History of Mary Gutzlaff (London, 1842).

Anstruther, *History of the Family of Anstruther* (Blackwood and Sons, 1923).

Beasley, *Great Britain and the Opening of Japan, 1834-1858* (London: Luzac & Co, 1951; repr. Routledge, 1995).

Bowers, *Sketches of Southwark Old and New* (London: Wesley & Son, 1902).

Churchill, *Observations on the Diseases Incident to Pregnancy and Childbed* (Dublin: Martin Keene & Son, 1840)

D'Arcy-Brown, *Chusan: The Forgotten Story of Britain's First Chinese Island* (Kenilworth: Brandram, 2013).

Druett, *Hen Frigates: Wives of Merchant Captains under Sail* (NY: Touchstone, 1999).

Factories Inquiry Commission. Supplementary Report, Part II, 1835.

First Annual Report of the National Society for Promoting the Education of the Poor in the Principles of the Established Church (London, 1812).

Forbes, *Five Years in China, from 1842 to 1847* (London: Bentley, 1848).

Graves, *1847-1922; the North Presbyterian Church, Buffalo, New York; a brief history prepared for the seventy-fifth anniversary, Dec. 29, 1922* (privately printed).

Harte and Ponting (eds), *Textile History & Economic History: Essays in Honour of Miss Julia de Lacy Mann* (Manchester: MUP, 1973).

Holden's Triennial Directory of 1805.

Lloyd's Register of British & Foreign Shipping (London: Cox & Sons).

sources and bibliography

Lucas, *Camp Life and Sport in South Africa: Experiences of Kaffir Warfare with the Cape Mounted Rifles* (1878).

McPherson, *Two Years in China: A Narrative of the Chinese Expedition from its Formation in April 1840 to the Treaty of Peace in August 1842* (London: Saunders & Otley 1843).

Morrell, *Captain's Wife: Narrative of a Voyage in the Schooner Antarctic* (Barnsley: Seaforth, 2012).

Ouchterlony, *The Chinese War: an account of all the operations of the British forces from the commencement to the treaty of Nanking* (London: Saunders & Otley 1844).

Yung Wing, *My Life in China and America* (NY: Henry Holt, 1909).

Newspapers

The Argus (London)
The Bombay Times
The Bristol Mercury
The Brooklyn Daily Eagle
The Christian Intelligencer of the Reformed Dutch Church, New York
The Commercial Daily List (London)
The Daily News (London)
The Eastern Star
The Englishman & Military Chronicle (Calcutta)
The Hampshire Advertiser & Salisbury Guardian
The Illustrated London News
The Illustrated Times (London)
The Ipswich Journal
Jackson's Oxford Journal
The Liverpool Mercury
Lloyd's List (London: W. Phillips)
The London Age
The Manchester Times & Gazette
The Mirror of Parliament (London)
The Morning Post (London)
The Norwich Mercury
The Newcastle Courant
The Newcastle Journal
The Royal Cornwall Gazette (Truro)
The Singapore Free Press (London)
The Standard (London)

(ii) Printed works in other languages

嶺田楓江《海外新話》 Mineta Fuko *Kaigai shinwa* (*New Stories from Overseas*)

嶺田楓江《海外新話拾遺》 Mineta Fuko *Kaigai shinwa shui* (*Gleanings from 'New Stories from Overseas'*)

齋藤竹堂《鴉片始末》 Saito Chikudo *Ahen shimatsu* (*Opium: Beginning to End*)

《光緒上虞縣志》 *Guangxu Shangyu xianzhi* (Shanyu County Annals, Guangxu reign period)

《寧波市志》 *Ningbo shizhi* (Ningbo City Annals, 1974 reprint)

(iii) Unpublished material

The National Archives, Kew

> *King's Bench and Fleet Prison Discharge Books and Prisoner Lists, 1734-1862* (PRIS 10/53).

> Strachan, *Diary of a residence on board the ship Scotland in Chusan harbour* (FO17/49(182)).

The British Library

> *'Up the Gulph'–the letters of Hugh Henry Monk, assistant surgeon RN, 1840-43* (Mss. Eur. C575/3).

> Major Thomas Pears' *Journals of Two Expeditions to China, 1840-41* (Mss. Eur. B368).

SOAS, London, Council for World Mission Archive

> The *Lockhart Correspondence* is held under MS.380645/1 and 'Missionary Archives, South China, inc. letters, 1832/33-1857, CWM.2'.

The National Maritime Museum, Greenwich, holds Edward Cree's diaries. Miles' article *Blind and Sighted Pioneer Teachers in 19th-Century China and India* (Birmingham, 1998) is available online through the Educational Resources Information Center. The handwritten rice-paper notes which were passed from Lieutenant Douglas and Captain Anstruther to Anne Noble during their imprisonment in Ningbo are now owned by an anonoymous collector in the US.

NOTES

Chapter 1

1 Written before more evidence on Anne's background came to light, *Chusan: The Forgotten Story of Britain's First Chinese Island* mistakenly refers to her as a Scotswoman (this is how she was described by Dr Edward Cree).

2 *Bristol Mercury*, 20/8/1842.

3 *Textile History & Economic History*, pp.179, 193; *Factories Inquiry Commission. Supplementary Report, Part II*, 1835, pp.102-5.

4 *Factories Inquiry Commission. Supplementary Report, Part II*, 1835.

5 *Ibid*, pp.102-5.

6 *First Annual Report of the National Society for Promoting the Education of the Poor in the Principles of the Established Church*, p.174.

7 *Ibid*, p.46.

8 *Norwich Mercury*, 6/4/1833.

9 *Holden's Triennial Directory of 1805*, v.2.

10 *Holden's Annual London and Country Directory of 1811*, vol.1.

11 *Morning Post*, 13/3/1810.

12 *Jackson's Oxford Journal*, 12/10/1811.

13 *King's Bench and Fleet Prison Discharge Books and Prisoner Lists, 1734-1862*, PRIS 10/53, p.286, discharged 5/10/1813.

14 *Newcastle Courant*, 1/12/1828.

15 *Liverpool Mercury*, 14/6/1833.

16 *Newcastle Courant*, 22/6/1833.

17 *The Christian Intelligencer*, Vol.IV (No.157), 3/8/1833.

18 *Newcastle Journal*, 31/8/1833.

19 E.g. *Morning Post*, 26/8/1826.

20 *Captain's Wife*, p.26.

Chapter 2

1 The 1841 Census records that Isabella Noble and the 3-year-old Annie were living together in George Street, North Shields; also, a letter written by Dr Lockhart in January 1841 (MS380645/1) mentions that Anne's sister-in-law was living in North Shields, so this is surely the same person.

2 E.g. *Hen Frigates*.

3 Clifford Ashley uses the term in *The Yankee Whaler* (1926), so it seems possible that it might have originated or clung on in North America.

4 *Hen Frigates*, p.94.

5 *Newcastle Courant*, 7/6/1839.

6 Many Western historians have written on the opium trade and the war it engendered: the most detailed history to date is Peter Ward Fay's highly readable *The Opium War: 1840-1842*; Julia Lovell's *The Opium War: Drugs, Dreams, and the Making of China* concentrates more on the lasting effect the conflict has had on China's self-image.

7 *Pekin Gazette*, 25/2/1838.

Chapter 3

1 'Up the Gulph'–the letters of
   Hugh Henry Monk, assistant
   surgeon RN, 1840-43 (British
   Library India Office Records,
   Mss. Eur. C575/3, 21/10/1840).
2 Letter from Color Serjeant
   J. Henderson to his father,
   19/10/1840, Acc. 9006-219-2-1,
   ©National Army Museum.
3 Englishman & Military
   Chronicle, 30/11/1840
   (letter of 2/10/1840).
4 National Archives, Registry
   of Shipping and Seamen:
   Index of Apprentices; Class:
   BT 150; Piece No. 18
   (Surnames K-Z, 1837-40).
5 Singapore Free Press, 25/2/1841.
6 Shangyu xianzhi (Shanyu
   County Annals, Guangxu
   reign period).
7 Ningbo shizhi (Ningbo City
   Annals, 1974 reprint) v.1, p.56.
8 My thanks to Rosemary
   Harden of the Fashion
   Museum in Bath for these
   details on Anne's clothing.
9 SOAS, Council for World
   Mission archive, MS.380645/1
   'Lockhart Correspondence'.

Chapter 5

1 Camp Life and Sport
   in South Africa.
2 Pears, Journals of Two
   Expeditions to China, p.93.
3 Two Years in China: A Narrative of the Chinese Expedition
   from its Formation in April
   1840 to the Treaty of Peace in
   August 1842, by D. McPherson.

4 Edward Cree's diaries,
   26/9/1840 (National Maritime
   Museum).
5 Ouchterlony, The Chinese War,
   p.192. It is unclear precisely
   who held this post during
   Anne's captivity: Li Shaofang
   was the taidao overseeing
   military affairs in the area
   around that time, and a man
   named Lu Zezhang seems
   to have held the civil post as
   taidao of Ningbo-Shaoxing.
6 Five Years in China, p.219.

Chapter 6

1 Strachan, Diary of a residence
   on board the ship Scotland in
   Chusan harbour, National Archives FO17/49(182) 19/9/1840.
2 Draft reply from Urgungga to
   Bremer, Daoguang 20/9/3.
3 Note to Mrs Noble, Ningbo
   prison, 8/10/1840.
4 Note to Mrs Noble, Ningbo
   prison, 12/10/1840.
5 Note to Mrs Noble, Ningbo
   prison, 19/10/1840.
6 Note to Mrs Noble, Ningbo
   prison, 12/10/1840.
7 Yung Wing, My Life in China
   and America, pp.3-4.
8 SOAS, 'Lockhart
   Correspondence', 19/1/1841.
9 Observations on the Diseases
   Incident to Pregnancy
   and Childbed, F Churchill
   (1840) p.107-8.
10 Note from Anstruther
   to Mrs Noble, Ningbo
   prison, undated.
11 Ibid.

12 Note from Anstruther
    to Mrs Noble, Ningbo
    prison, 17/11/1840.
13 Details from various notes
    from Anstruther to Mrs Noble,
    Ningbo prison, Nov-Dec 1840.
14 *Two Years in China: A Narra-
    tive of the Chinese Expedition
    from its Formation in April
    1840 to the Treaty of Peace in
    August 1842*, by D. McPherson.

Chapter 7
1   The opera was still being per-
    formed in the 1840s: see e.g.
    London Age, 9/10/1842 (at
    the Theatre Royal, Covent
    Garden).
2   *The Englishman & Military
    Chronicle*, letter dated
    17/12/1840.
3   *Eastern Star*, 21/2/1841, Blon-
    del's answers to questions put
    to him by Gutzlaff, 4/1/1841.
4   *The Englishman & Military
    Chronicle*, 22/3/1841 (let-
    ter from Anstruther in
    Ningbo, 14/1/1841).

Chapter 8
1   SOAS, Council for World
    Mission archive, microfiched
    correspondence, 'Missionary
    Archives, South China,
    inc. letters, 1832/33-1857,
    CWM.2'. Letter of 27/2/1841.
2   Letter to Anne from Jane
    Hobson, Macau, July 1841,
    private collection.
3   *Ipswich Journal*, 4/9/1841.
4   Reprint in *Bristol Mercury*,
    7/8/1841, of a letter written
    on HMS *Blenheim* off

    Anunghoy, 10/3/1841.
5   Letter from Dr Lockhart
    in Macau, 2/4/1841.
6   Letter from Dr Lockhart
    in Macau, 19/4/1841.
7   Letter from Dr Lockhart
    in Macau, 23/4/1841.
8   Letter from Dr Lockhart
    in Macau, 23/6/1841.
9   *Ipswich Journal*, 4/9/1841.
10 *Bombay Times*, 27/9/1841.
11 *Ibid.*
12 *Lloyd's List*, 1841.
13 Advert, *Manchester Times
    & Gazette*, 18/4/1840.
14 *Commercial Daily
    List*, 21/1/1842.
15 *Morning Post*, 21/12/1841.
16 *Morning Post*, 30/12/1841.
17 *Illustrated London
    News*, 13/8/1842.
18 Private letter to Anne
    Noble, 27/3/1842.
19 *Ibid.*
20 National Archives,
    ADM 45/15/618.
21 *Mirror of Parliament*,
    Second Session of 1841,
    p.295, 17/9/1841.
22 *The Argus*, 31/12/1842.
23 *The Standard*, 1/8/1842.
24 Ouchterlony, *The
    Chinese War*, p.192.
25 McPherson, *Two Years
    in China*, p.49.
26 Ouchterlony, *The
    Chinese War*, p.192ff.
27 *Morning Post*, 17/8/1842.
28 E.g. *Morning Post*, 14/4/1846.
29 Private letter to Anne
    Noble, 29/9/1842.
30 National Archives,

ADM 45/15/618.

31 Bowers, *Sketches of Southwark Old and New* (1902).

32 1841 and 1851 census data.

33 *Bristol Mercury*, 20/12/1845.

34 'Brass band': *Hampshire Advertiser & Salisbury Guardian*, 29/4/1848.

35 *Bristol Mercury*, 20/12/1845.

36 See e.g. *Jackson's Oxford Journal*, 5/6/1847; *Hampshire Advertiser & Salisbury Guardian*, 25/3, 29/4 and 10/6/1848; *The Royal Cornwall Gazette, Falmouth Packet, & General Advertiser*, 3/5, 3/24, 30/8, 11/10/1850.

37 *Jackson's Oxford Journal*, 5/6/1847.

38 Beasley, *Great Britain and the Opening of Japan*, p.37. The account by Saito Chikudo was called *Opium: Beginning to End* (*Ahen shimatsu*).

39 Dower, *The Opium War in Japanese Eyes* (part of MIT's Visualizing Cultures project).

40 Mineta Fuko's *Kaigai shinwa*.

41 *Kaigai shinwa shui*.

42 Dower (above, n.39).

Chapter 9

1 *Brooklyn Daily Eagle*, 22/2/1845, citing *Journal of Commerce*, 9/1/1845.

2 *Brooklyn Daily Eagle*, 31/3/1856, has a notice inserted by a Thomas Reynolds, describing his property's site. The 1855 NY State Census records the family and how long they had been in the city.

3 Thirty-three of Otis' letters to Annie form the 'Otis Moody—Annie F. Noble Collection' in the Lincoln Financial Foundation Collection at Allen County Public Library, Fort Wayne, IN.

4 The Buffalo Architecture and History website has details of Charles' businesses and his home in Cottage Street.

5 Graves, *1847-1922; the North Presbyterian Church, Buffalo, New York; a brief history prepared for the seventy-fifth anniversary, Dec. 29, 1922.*

6 Anstruther, *History of the Family of Anstruther* (Blackwood and Sons, 1923), p.31.

7 'Indian Mail', *Daily News*, 19/6/1856.

8 *Hampshire Advertiser & Salisbury Guardian*, 13/7/1844.

9 *The Standard*, 23/3/1852; also *O'Byrne's Naval Biographical Dictionary*.

10 13/4/1842.

11 National Maritime Museum, Masters' Certificates, nos 81,670 and 53,716. The latter confirms that by 1860 Twizell had served as an apprentice, mate, and master for 24 years in the coasting and foreign trades.

12 *Newcastle Courant*, 4/2/1853.

13 *Newcastle Courant*, 30/4/1858.

14 National Archives, FO17/82(13) (letter by Robert Thom).

15 *The Blind and their Books*; *The History of Mary Gutzlaff*; Miles, *Blind and*

    Sighted Pioneer Teachers.
16 *The Female Missionary
Intelligencer 1857*, No.44, 4:41.
17 *Fortieth Annual Report
of the London Society for
Teaching the Blind to Read*,
28/5/1878, pp.15-16.
18 *Illustrated Times*, 26/6/1858.
19 *London & its Environs*
(Edwards, 1927).

Lightning Source UK Ltd.
Milton Keynes UK
UKOW02f1927280616

277289UK00001B/8/P